COMMUNICATION SERIES

Assertiveness Skills

12 Action Steps to Create Visibility and Take Charge of Your Life

Written by Gail Cohen
Edited by National Press Publications

NATIONAL PRESS PUBLICATIONS

A Division of Rockhurst College Continuing Education Center, Inc.
6901 West 63rd Street • P.O. Box 2949 • Shawnee Mission, Kansas 66201-1349
1-800-258-7248 • 1-913-432-7757

Dedication

For "T"

National Press Publications endorses nonsexist language. In an effort to make this handbook clear, consistent and easy to read, we have used "he" throughout the odd-numbered chapters and "she" throughout the even-numbered chapters. The copy is not intended to be sexist.

Assertiveness Skills: *12 Action Steps to Create Visibility and Take Charge of Your Life*

Published by National Press Publications, Inc.
Copyright 1998 National Press Publications, Inc.
A Division of Rockhurst College Continuing Education Center, Inc.

Printed in the United States of America

5 6 7 8 9 10

ISBN 1-55852-227-1

Table of Contents

1 MAKING ASSERTIVENESS YOUR LIFE CHOICE

"It is choice not chance that determines destiny."

— Anonymous

What a great decision you just made. By reading this book you made the choice to improve your life. It doesn't get any better than that!

What's in It for You?

Here are the 10 benefits available to you when you implement the methods discussed in this book. At the completion of this book, you will be able to:

1. Recognize passive, aggressive, and assertive behavior in yourself and others

2. Determine which behavior is appropriate for a given situation

3. Feel comfortable about honestly expressing yourself, including saying no

4. Deal successfully with a wide variety of behaviors that differ from yours

5. Practice the Three Rs for personal assertive success

6. Know and conquer the number one enemy of assertive behavior

7. Take the four steps to get outside your comfort zone — and enjoy the trip!

8. Comfortably deliver the Five-Part Assertive Conversation to handle any confrontation

9. Control the five life areas that allow you to take leadership in your personal and professional life

10. Adapt the four methods to ensure your continuing assertive success

Now, let's get down to the business of you *taking charge of your life!*

How Do I Become More Assertive?

Are you looking for assertiveness here? You won't find it.

That's right. You won't find your assertiveness in this book, or any other book, audio or video, or from any other person. That is because you already have all you need. You have an abundant, infinite, unlimited supply of assertiveness. You were born with it, no one gave it to you and no one can take it away. That's your first lesson.

Lesson #1: You have all the assertiveness you need

What this book *will* do is help you use that innate supply of assertiveness. The book will show you how to tap into your assertiveness at will; to manage your own life and influence the lives of others. But your success will depend on your approach.

Most people approach a self-help book in one of three ways. Which was your approach?

Approach #1:	"Oh, I suppose I better read this – but I'd rather be sailing!"
Approach #2:	"What a great opportunity this is: I can't wait to get into this book!"
Approach #3:	"This'll never work."

If you chose number one, thanks for you honesty. If you chose number two, I'd like to meet you. If you chose number three, you're right. It won't work for you.

Did you ever say to someone else, "You make me mad" — or just think it? Of course, we all have. But who really makes you mad? You do. The other person creates negative space and you step right in it and then blame them for your choice! And that's your second lesson.

Lesson #2: It's your choice to tap into your assertive supply

You will get everything you need to make assertive choices in your life right here in this book — all the tips and techniques, words and wisdom, diagrams and dialogue methods and models. Then it's up to you. You will make the choice to use them and in doing so to take charge of your life.

What Assertiveness Is and Isn't

Assertiveness is not a bunch of techniques strung together like beads on a necklace. It is not something that one does, it is something that one is. It is an approach, a life choice, a way of being. It is language, demeanor, attitude, goals, desires. It is caring for oneself and others. More specifically …

Assertiveness Is Not:

- Manipulative techniques ·

  Tricks that get people to say or do what you want are temporary at best. At worst, they create ill will and fail to teach long-term behavior changes that generate positive results and relationships.

- Mindless power moves

  Bullying tactics, language and body movement intended to intimidate will drive others to avoid or ignore the perpetrator. Individuality suffers and progress slows.

- Difficult to learn or master

  Everyone has the assertive potential. As you have already learned, it only requires your choice to use it. If it seems to come easy for some people, it's because they have tapped deeper into their assertive potential. You can do that too — you already have by reading this.

- Gender- or culturally-specific

Regardless of whether you are male or female, young or old, and regardless of where you are from, you can tap into your assertive potential. You will learn body movements that will signal others that you are an assertive person.

Assertiveness Is:

- Stress-relieving

When assertiveness is your choice you rid yourself of the "shoulda's." "I shoulda said what I thought" or "I shoulda told him off." Instead, you can feel good about yourself and be proud of your self-control. And part of your learning process will be to feel comfortable with yourself after you have made the assertive choice.

- A positive and attractive human characteristic

People admire and respect those who state their position with clarity and confidence; who say what they mean without unnecessarily injuring others; and who maintain dignity while neither showing exaggerated aggressiveness or victimizing themselves. In the long term, people like those who say no when they mean it.

- Needs-satisfying

In order to get what you want you must let others know what you want. For example, you need to tell people that you want privacy, more money, less work, respect and acknowledgment of your ideas and your work. You must tell others that you're tired, angry, frustrated or happy — if their not knowing is creating a problem for you. They will respond. You get what you want most often by asking for it — it's as simple as that!

- Healthy

  To obsess about what you want and need, to complain and gripe about your problems while not doing anything about it is a drain on your mental, physical and emotional well-being. Assertive behavior means not taking a problem to those who will agree but rather to those who can do something about it. Assertive behavior means not complaining about the same problem day after day, month after month, year after year. Assertive behavior is healthier for the mind, the body, the soul.

Tapping into Your Assertive Supply

The Passive-Aggressive Continuum

← →

Passive   **Aggressive**

Case Study 1: The Report

Franz has worked overtime three days this week. He made plans with his wife and children to go away for the weekend. It's Friday, 5:00 p.m. and his family is home, packed and waiting for him. Franz's supervisor, Helen, walks in.

"Franz, I need you to do this report before you leave. It should only take a couple of hours. Jan made such a mess of it last month, I want you to handle it this month. I'd do it myself but I have plans tonight. Thanks a bunch!" Helen then glances at her watch and says, "Gotta run!"

Franz slams down his briefcase — after Helen leaves. He calls his wife, who is not happy, and proceeds to complete the report. He leaves it on Helen's desk three hours later and goes home.

If you were Franz, what would you do? The same? Different? If different, what?

Case Study 2: The Microwave Oven

Eva purchased a microwave oven from a large department store. Two days after the warranty ran out the unit stopped working. She called the store and demanded to have her warranty honored. Her volume was loud, her tone abusive.

"You're a bunch of thieves," she told the customer service department. "You probably have a built-in trigger for these things to stop working when you're off the hook."

She continued, "Well, I'm not going to stand for this. I'm reporting you to the Chamber of Commerce." She then used some foul language and hung up. The customer service rep never got to say one word after his opening statement, "How can I help you?"

If you were Eva, what would you do? The same? Different? If different, what?

The Assertive Solution

You probably would agree that Franz in Case Study 1 exhibited inappropriate passive behavior and that in Case Study 2, Eva showed excessive aggression. It's pretty easy to identify extremes in the Passive-Aggressive Continuum.

It is a little more difficult to decide how these situations should have been handled. And even more difficult to do it. Let's take the first question: How would you handle your supervisor if you were Franz?

You might have said that you would have stood up to her, politely but forcefully. Something like the following:

"Helen, I have worked three nights this week and I'm exhausted. I have plans this weekend too, with my family and they're waiting for me. I will be happy to do this report on Monday, or I can suggest someone else on the team who can do it just as well. I'll even assist Jan next month so she can handle this better in the future. But right now I do need to leave."

What about Eva? How would you handle the situation if it were your microwave?

You probably said you wouldn't use foul language, an abusive tone or have raised your voice. You might have said, "I have been a good customer of yours for 10 years. Since it's only two days after the warranty expired, I expect you to honor it."

If that failed, you perhaps would have asked for a supervisor or even gone to the manufacturer.

Assuming there are no extenuating circumstances, each of those new ways of handling Franz's and Eva's problem could be considered assertive and certainly more appropriate than their way in the case studies.

But how do you actually do it? What propels you to actually say the words without falling apart or suffering guilt pains afterward? I say it's the Assertive Belief.

The Assertive Belief

The Assertive Belief keeps you or me or anyone else on track during the encounter, and without anxiety afterward. It is a belief in rights — yours and others.

Those who are inappropriately passive, like Franz in Case Study 1, have an exaggerated view of others' rights and a limited view of their own rights.

Those who are inappropriately aggressive, like Eva in Case Study 2, have an exaggerated view of their own rights and a limited view of the rights of others.

What were Franz's rights? He had a right to take time off, to refuse to work overtime, to state his opinion. What were Helen's, his supervisor's, rights? She had a right to ask Franz to work extra hours.

In Eva's case she had a right to request extending the warranty; she had a right to express her dissatisfaction. The customer service rep also had rights, perhaps to explain the store's policy and to refuse or accept the customer's request.

When in a confrontational situation, your comfort, your ease in stating your opinion and your satisfaction with your behavior later on will be enormously improved if you consider who has rights and what they are.

You have all the assertiveness you need. Making the choice to tap into that limitless supply is done by a well-balanced consideration of your rights and the rights of others.

Review and Reinforcement

Key Points in This Chapter

- You have already made a positive assertive choice to enhance your life.

- The first two lessons of assertive behavior:

    1. You have all the assertiveness you need

    2. It is your choice to tap into that supply

- Assertiveness is not innate to any gender, culture or age group.

- Assertiveness is healthy, a positive attribute, and easy to learn.

- The Assertive Belief is a belief in your rights balanced with a belief in the rights of others. Staying focused before and after an encounter depends on your willingness to develop that belief.

- You will gain at least 10 benefits by completing this book and implementing the methods suggested.

Your Personal Assertive Bill of Rights

1. You have the right to think of yourself first since your opinion of yourself is more important than others' opinion of you.

2. You have the right to manage your own life, but no one else's.

3. You have the right to stand up for yourself, after all, you are responsible for your own actions.

4. You have the right to try to influence others, but not to expect others to always do what you want.

5. You have the right to behave as you choose as long as that behavior does not hurt or deprive others of their rights.

6. You have the right to say, "I don't know," "I don't understand," "I need time to think." You need not give more explanation than that.

7. You have the right to say no and not feel guilty.

Skill Practice

Write down a situation you would like to confront. It can be personal or professional:

List three of your rights and three of the other person's or persons' rights in the above situation:

My rights are:

1.

2.

3.

Their rights are:

1.

2.

3.

Reflections

Keeper Korner

Write down the most important point you learned or relearned in this chapter:

_____

_____

_____

2 DISCOVERING WHO YOU ARE AND WHY YOU BEHAVE AS YOU DO

"The longest journey begins with the first step."

— Ancient Chinese proverb

This chapter begins what will be the structure, the foundation and the daily support of your assertive life — *12 Positive Action Steps for Taking Charge of Your Life!*

The first two action steps teach you to look within, to develop intrapersonal skills that will strengthen the core that is you. When you complete this chapter, you will be able to:

- Talk to and about yourself in ways that empower

- Build a strong self-image

- Adopt three ways to develop self-esteem from within

- Use verbal and nonverbal cues to demonstrate your self-worth

- Be passive, aggressive or assertive as the situation demands

- Realize the three advantages to developing assertive behavior

- Recognize eight situations where you should not be passive

- Recognize eight situations where you should not be aggressive

Positive Action Step #1: Like Me!

Did you know that 80 percent of the conversations you will have in your life will be with yourself? That means that how you have been talking to yourself all these years has formed your opinion of you — your self-esteem. Your self-esteem will determine to the greatest extent possible how well you are able to tap into your assertiveness, and how successful you are with interpersonal relationships.

> *The greater your self-esteem,*
>
> *The greater your ability to lead, motivate and persuade.*
>
> *The lower your self-esteem,*
>
> *The less your ability to lead, motivate and persuade.*

The Process of Self-Esteem

If you are saying to yourself right now, "Well that's good, because I've already done my self-esteem — so that's complete," you are mistaken. You can't "have done" self-esteem. It's not an event, it's a process. It's like hair or skin or teeth. If you don't take care, it dulls, dries up, erodes. But the good news is self-esteem is learned behavior. You can even see it!

Self-Esteem Is Observable

Think of the winners in your life. You can spot a winner or loser 20 feet away. Think of how the winners you know approach you. Notice how they greet you, hold out their hand to shake if it's appropriate. Notice how winners enunciate their names clearly and distinctly. You never have to ask a winner to repeat his or her name. They ask you your name and show a genuine interest in you. Winners present themselves with pride and confidence and they want to know about you as well.

Those are the observable clues to a winner, a person with strong self-esteem. To show you are a winner, give strong signals through voice, tone and body movement. Your entire verbal and nonverbal presence needs to say, "I like me!" This signals others to treat you with the respect you deserve. To make sure this behavior is long-lasting, you must reinforce from within.

Three Ways to Develop Self-Esteem from Within

Case Study: Jelly Suit

You are on your way to an important meeting. You have dressed carefully, you are looking good. You're running late so you decide to balance your car keys, jacket, a cup of coffee and toast with jelly as you run out to the car. You trip. Everything comes crashing to the ground, but not before the coffee and jelly have made tracks down the front of your suit and come to rest on top of your highly polished shoes. What do you say to yourself?

"What an idiot I am. How could I do that? I always do these dumb things. Now I can either be late or be jellied for the meeting. How could I be so stupid?"

How demoralizing that is, how degrading, how inhibiting. You probably wouldn't speak to a stranger like that. Would you? Let alone your best friend.

What would your best friend say to you at that moment? Would she or he console and offer suggestions and shift from the problem to the solution?

"I know you're upset but you didn't do it on purpose. You were just excited and anxious to be on time. Come on, we'll clean you up and get you on the road in no time. Tell the people at your meeting about what happened. Everyone can identify with something like this. It will be an ice breaker."

Isn't that more empowering language? Aren't you more apt to address and rectify the situation quickly and successfully with those words ringing in your ears? Well, you can be that best friend. In fact, shouldn't you be your own best friend? If not you, who?

> *Be your own best friend.*

When you make a mistake, forgive yourself and offer alternative actions, "I don't like the way I did that, I'm going to do it differently next time," or "That wasn't like me. I'll find a better way," or "So I made a mistake — welcome to the human race!"

Case Study: The Branch Office

You have just opened a new branch office. You stayed at work late and worked weekends for two months to meet the deadline. You organized the team and they worked well under your direction. There were a few glitches but the few there were you handled efficiently. At the grand opening someone turns to you and says,

"Great job. You must have put in a lot of time to get this thing accomplished." You smile and say, "Oh, it was nothing, really, my team did most of it."

Others will only respect you as much as you respect yourself. They get three cues from you. How do you respond to praise? Do you minimize your accomplishments as in this case study? Do you nullify compliments? When someone says you look good, do you say, "Me? I'm having the worst hair day of my life!" or do you simply say, "Thank you."

> *Speak kindly and honestly about yourself.*

How much better would you and the other person feel in the case study above if you had responded instead with, "Thank you. I did put in a lot of time because it was important to all of us and I had a great team that also worked hard to reach our goal."

Case Study: Work or Play?

It's Friday and your desk as usual is piled high with work. You've been on a treadmill all week trying to balance family and work. Giving to each what they need and want from you. That's okay because you enjoy giving. But you are a little bushed right now. As you reach for the stack of papers you plan to take home and work on tonight, your phone rings. It's someone very special in your life asking you out to dinner. You'd really love to go — but you have all this work. What will you do?

You probably have family obligations and work responsibilities that demand a great deal of your time as in this case study but there is a third obligation; and that's you. Living an assertive life means taking time for you — time for fun, for thought, for calm, for self. Giving in to your personal wants and needs will replenish and refresh all areas of your life.

> *Take time for you.*

You will be more willing to give to others when you know that you take time for you as well. The most creative results come from those who balance their loyalties between their organization, their family and themselves.

Positive Action Step #2: Know Me

In the last chapter you saw the Passive-Aggressive Continuum, examples of the extremes and how to use the Assertive Belief to adopt an assertive attitude. This time you will look at your behavior in all three modes: passive, aggressive and assertive. When each is appropriate and when it is not.

Passive Behavior

What are the observable characteristics of passive behavior? Think about yourself and answer the following questions.

When you are in a passive mode:

- How do you walk?

- How do you stand?

- How is your tone of voice?

- What are your facial expressions? Where do you look?

- When in a group what is your contribution to the conversations?

- What you do with your hands?

- What is the volume of your voice?

- What are your decision-making methods?

You probably described your passive actions as slow, conservative, low-volume, withdrawn, cautious. Is it sometimes okay to be passive? Of course it is. It is appropriate when you are learning, sitting in a movie, listening to someone who is distraught, when you are unsure and the decision carries serious consequences — lots of times.

Is it sometimes not okay to adopt a passive mode? Also true. And yet most people would agree that they have taken a passive mode at times and regretted it. Can you think of a time when you were passive and you were sorry later that you had not taken a more assertive role? Here are eight situations when it is not appropriate to be passive, followed by examples to help you move out of passive to more appropriate behavior.

Do not be passive when you:

1. Are in an urgent situation

There is no time to be silent or slow. Speak in a volume and tone so that others can hear you and understand the urgency, use demonstrative body movements and facial expressions that convey meaning.

Example: "This is an urgent situation, we need to act now to avoid harmful consequences ..."

2. Have unique information

If the information that you have is different or unique, offer it. If what you know could change or alter discussions of those around you, give them that information. If it's important, press to make sure they understand it as clearly as you do.

Example: "I have some information that will help you with this discussion ..."

3. Are being hurt, neglected or ignored

No one has the right to treat you badly. If you are being treated in ways that you believe are unfair or unjustified, tell those who can and will help you. Whether it is an insulting remark or physical abuse, you have the right to stop it.

Example: "I am not being treated with the dignity I deserve. I need you to stop that now and be more respectful of me ..."

4. Will feel regret or guilt later

If you think, "I should speak up, I'll be sorry if I don't," you probably will. The pain of confrontation now is much less than the long dragged-out pain of regret later.

Example: "This situation is not acceptable to me. Here's what I believe will work better ..."

5. Are being counted on by others

If others count on you, don't let them down. Rise above any shyness or uncertainty by knowing that if you try and make a mistake, others will forgive you but they are less apt to forgive if you don't try at all.

Example: "You are relying on me to provide input. I'm not sure if I have everything you need but here's what I have so far ..."

6. Can help yourself or others

Don't wait for others to step in if you can solve a problem or help somebody. Too many people sit back and say, "Someone else will do it," very often no one will. An assertive life means taking the initiative, not waiting to see if someone else will.

Example: "Someone needs to take action here and I'm willing to do it. Here's what I think should be done ..."

7. Are not sure what to do

If you are unclear, ask. If you don't know, seek out the answer. More opportunities are missed, successes not achieved, more happiness unrealized and more friendships broken because someone was unwilling to ask why or how.

Example: "I know you've described the process but I'm still not clear and I want to do a good job. Could you explain again how ..."

8. Are not being taken seriously

You have the right to be taken seriously. If others find you amusing when that was not your intent, or if your thoughts and ideas are met with sarcasm or ignored, tell the perpetrator that you are serious about your suggestion and expect it to be taken as such.

Example: "This is very important to me, and I've given it a great deal of thought. I would like you to consider it in that light ..."

In summary, passive behavior is not intrinsically bad or good. To be an assertive person, your behavior — words, tone, actions — must match the situation. Let's look at the polar opposite: aggressive behavior.

Aggressive Behavior

As you did with passive behavior, consider the observable characteristics of aggressive behavior. Think about yourself and answer the following questions.

When you are in an aggressive mode:

- How do you walk?

- How do you stand?

- How is your tone of voice?

- What are your facial expressions? Where do you look?

- When in a group what is your contribution to the conversations?

- What do you do with your hands?

- What is the volume of your voice?

- What are your decision-making methods?

You probably described your aggressive actions as fast, impulsive, high volume, spontaneous, outgoing. As it was with passive behavior, is it sometimes okay to be aggressive? Again, yes. It is appropriate when you are in a leadership position, playing tennis, motivating someone to act, when you are sure and the decision carries serious consequences, in an emergency, lots of times.

Is it sometimes not okay to adopt an aggressive mode? Yes. And yet most people would agree that they have taken an aggressive mode at times and regretted it. Can you think of a time when you were aggressive and you were sorry later that you acted like Attila the Hun? Here are eight situations when it is not appropriate to be aggressive, followed by examples to help you move out of aggressive to more appropriate behavior.

Do not be aggressive when you:

1. Are not sure of the outcome

Use caution even in urgent situations if you are not sure of the results of your aggressive behavior. There are risks involved with any action, just reduce your risk by giving as much thought as you can without danger to life or property.

Example: "I believe we should take this action, but there are some considerations; for example ..."

2. See big risks and small gains

When your actions will put you and others at risk and what you stand to gain is minimal, take care with your behavior. You may want to adopt a more careful approach.

Example: "This is a gamble, we stand to lose a great deal and I don't see that we will get much in return ..."

3. Need to let others develop and grow

If you are in a position to allow others to step out and try their own leadership and other skills, there are times when you must pull back and let the spotlight shine elsewhere. If you are a parent or team leader, manager or supervisor, you perhaps have many occasions where your passive behavior would be good for another, for the team or family and good for you.

Example: "It's your turn to take over. I'll be here to support you if you need me ..."

4. Observe things working fine without you

When things are going well, be grateful. That's not the time to take over. That's the time to sit back and enjoy. If you were the catalyst take pride in what you did. If you had nothing to do with it, be happy for others.

Example: "Things are going so well for you, I don't think I can add a thing. Good luck …"

5. Are faced with a sensitive or emotional situation

If someone is upset or there is a highly charged emotional encounter, don't counterattack with aggressive behavior. Be calm, be quiet, listen, comment as needed but otherwise adopt a passive mode in words, tone and body.

Example: "I know you're upset about this. Tell me what this is about and what you'd like me to do …"

6. Are not involved and cannot add value

There are times, even urgent times, when your involvement will only add to the problem. An excellent example is an accident on the highway, when emergency vehicles and personnel are in control and drivers still pull over or slow down to look and do nothing but add difficulty to an already tragic situation. If you can't help and it's not your business, stay away.

Example: "I can see this is not my business and there's nothing I can add …"

7. Will intimidate others unnecessarily

Some people use aggressive behavior to scare others into action. You might be able to come up with a situation where that is desirable. But if your only goal is to intimidate, don't. It might be faster and easier to aggressively push your point forward — especially if you have the authority. But long term you are better off finding other, more functional ways to accomplish the same thing.

Example: "I don't mean to intimidate you. I want you to do this because you want to. Let me explain why I think it's best …"

8. May destroy a relationship that is working

Good relationships, whether with coworkers, friends or family are the most precious experiences we humans have. Treat them that way. If a relationship is working but requires, as they all do, some maintenance now and then, don't undermine the foundation with unnecessary aggression. Go gently. Treat it like the most prized possession you have; it may be.

Example: "Our relationship is more important than this current disagreement we're having. Let's see if we can work on it together to find a solution ..."

As you saw with passive behavior, aggressiveness is not intrinsically bad or good. It depends on the situation. So where does assertiveness fit in? If aggression is far to the right of the Passive-Aggressive Continuum and passive is far to the left, assertive must be right in between. Right? Wrong!

Finding the Assertive Place

Assertiveness is not a specific place on the Passive-Aggressive Continuum; it is any place on it. Being assertive means finding the right place on the continuum for the optimum results. And that is the definition of assertiveness.

> *Assertiveness is finding the right place*
>
> *On the Passive-Aggressive Continuum.*

The observable characteristics of assertive can be a loud voice, fast movement and quick decisions as you would see a firefighter adopt at the scene of a fire. Or it could be the soft gentle voice of a parent calming a crying and scared child. Assertiveness is knowing the behavior to adopt that gets you and others the results you want by using the best possible method. How do you know what that behavior is? By using the Assertive Belief you learned in the last chapter.

In other words, what are the rights of others and what are your rights? In the firefighter example I gave just now, firefighters know they are in charge and have the right to tell others what to do. They know they can provide support and that the situation is urgent.

In the case of the parent, he or she knows that the child, as a child, has a right to feel scared. This parent perhaps believes that his or her rights of anger or frustration are superseded by the child's right to cry.

Develop this ability and you will find the right place on the Passive-Aggressive Continuum time after time. Your advantages in finding appropriate behavior every time are many. But these three are the most meaningful of all.

Three Advantages of an Assertive Position

1. Control

You cannot control anyone but yourself. However, you can enormously influence a wide range of behaviors by controlling your emotions. And you can influence the situation and outcome by controlling your reactions.

Case Study: Debbie's Mess

Debbie is a teenager whose room looks like a hurricane and a tornado both hit with full force. Her mother wants Debbie to keep her room neat. She cannot change Debbie, only Debbie can do that. But Debbie's mother does have at least three options to influence the results she gets.

Option 1:

She can yell and holler and otherwise demonstrate her anger, in which case, Debbie will probably do a cursory job in her room just to get Mom off her case. Next week her room will look exactly the same as it did before the clean-up.

Option 2:

She can ignore it, pretend it doesn't exist, and seethe underneath. Debbie gets off — sort of — because Mom will make little verbal digs and will not be pleasant to be around. The room doesn't change and neither does Debbie.

Option 3:

She can have a conversation with Debbie in which she controls her own emotions, suggests what rights each of them have within the family, and asks Debbie what additional rights she would like to have that would make it worth keeping her room clean on a regular basis.

Will Option 3 work? Maybe. It will depend on the follow-through Debbie's Mom is willing to commit to. But it certainly has a better chance than either 1 or 2. And it is a good example for Debbie that neither aggressive emotion nor passive avoidance is good for a relationship. Good training, Mom!

2. Time management

Time is one of the most important elements in your assertive life. If you don't have control over your time, someone else does. Finding the right behavior for a situation and your willingness to invest up front will allow you to manage your time better.

Case Study: Mavis Objects

Ron needs to give Mavis a project. He knows she hates this project and has her own ideas on how it should be done. But Ron's boss is pressing him for results and he just doesn't have time for Mavis' complaints. He has some two options.

Option 1:

Ron can draw on his authority, he is the boss, and tell Mavis, "I know you don't like this but I can't deal with that now. I need it done and I need it done fast. Just do it."

How is Mavis likely to do the project? Without enthusiasm, making avoidable errors. Ron may have to speak to her several times, may have to get someone else involved and may even have to finish it himself. Has he saved time? What little time he saved in the beginning is long gone during the project implementation.

Option 2:

Ron can tell his boss that Mavis has some ideas on how to do the project more efficiently and get the boss's agreement that it's worth the time investment to get buy-in up front. He can then ask Mavis her thoughts on the project, "Mavis, I know you don't like this project, but it needs to be done. If you have some suggestions, I'll be glad to listen and give the okay on anything I can. For the rest I'll do my best to explain why and how we need to do it."

With that up-front investment of time, Mavis will likely do the project with interest and ownership. Ron will be free to remove himself and can concentrate on his own work. His up-front investment gives him big returns long term.

3. Ability to deal with different behaviors

Those who insist on behaving in singular ways, refusing to develop new skills to manage people have committed themselves to a narrow world. They will never experience, as you will, the personal satisfaction of being able and willing to change behavior to meet the needs of individuals and situations.

The next chapter will show you how to deal with a variety of behaviors to get the results you want.

Review and Reinforcement

Key Points in This Chapter

- The greater your self-esteem, the greater your ability to lead, motivate and persuade.

- The lower your self-esteem, the less your ability to lead, motivate and persuade.

- How you talk to yourself, about yourself and how you treat yourself more than anything else determines the strength of your self-esteem.

- Your verbal and nonverbal clues give messages to others on how you wish to be treated by others.

- Passive and aggressive behavior is not intrinsically bad.

- Assertiveness is finding the right place on the passive-aggressive continuum for a given situation.

- The benefits of assertive behavior are: control, time management and the ability to deal with many different behaviors.

Skill Practice

In dealing with others, which style reflects you best? (Check all the characteristics that describe your interactive style.)

Autocratic Style

_____ Says little unless something is wrong

_____ Usually not interested in others' ideas

_____ Holds information until the last minute

_____ Changes demands unexpectedly

_____ Is sometimes hard to talk to

_____ Discourages risk-taking

_____ Sets objectives for others

_____ Makes personal judgments on others' performance standards

Developmental Style

_____ Considers all ideas

_____ Allows reasonable margin of error

_____ Tries to help others learn from mistakes

_____ Has consistently high expectations

_____ Encourages growth, change, new directions

_____ Helps people understand the objectives of their jobs

_____ Allows people to make their own commitments

_____ Sets objectives with people

Reflections

Whether you manage people, systems or products or just manage yourself, whether you supervise at work or at home, the developmental style will be rewarding for you and enhance the lives of those around you. Work toward eliminating the checks in your autocratic style and increasing those of your developmental style.

Keeper Korner

Write down the most important point you learned or relearned in this chapter.

_____

_____

_____

3 ASSERTIVELY HANDLING DIFFICULT PEOPLE AND TOUGH SITUATIONS

"There are no difficult people — just different people."

— "Coach Joe" Gilliam

For good or for ill, we do not live or work in isolation. We must interact with others on a daily, even hourly basis. Your ability to manage behaviors, to assert yourself with people who are different from you will determine how successful you are in your personal and professional life.

This chapter will cover the next step in your *12 Positive Action Steps for Taking Charge of Your Life*. When you complete this chapter you will be able to:

- Understand the four primary behavioral styles

- Recognize the characteristics and communication style of each

- Successfully assert yourself with each style

- Identify your behavioral style

- Manage your style so that it interacts well with each of the others

Positive Action Step #3: Know Them

Abraham Lincoln once said, "I don't like that man, I think I'll get to know him better." Many times when we think we don't like people or find them difficult to get along with, it is actually that we don't understand them. Once you understand another, you can find ways to interact assertively and successfully. And, even if you never end up as best friends, you are able to work together and even socialize without the pain of conflict.

First we will look at two dimensions of the human character, then the four profiles or behaviors that are created out of those dimensions. The next step will be to look at ways to deal with each of them — from the autocratic know-it-all to those who are so nonresponsive you can't get them to express how they feel or what they want.

Whether you have a "different" person who is your boss, your employee, a coworker, your husband, wife, child or just someone you know, you can make your interaction with that person more satisfying and more successful.

Two Behavioral Dimensions

EASY-GOING   **DOMINANT**

←――――――――――――――――――――――――――――――――――→

If you took a horizontal continuum and labeled the far left "easy-going" and the right "dominant" you could identify everyone you know as having a primary style somewhere along that line. For example, the people who are very relaxed most of the time, quiet, patient, often seem deep in thought you might place on the "easy-going" side. Much like the passive end of the Passive-Aggressive Continuum.

Those who are more straightforward in their language and actions, who speak up at meetings, are definitive in their body movements and decisions you would place on the "dominant" side, similar to the aggressive end of the Passive-Aggressive Continuum. Others you might place in the middle or toward the left or toward the right.

What you are doing is recognizing the *ASSERTIVE DIMENSION* of the people in your life. You know from the previous chapter that this is neither good nor bad, it is simply behavior. We need to look at the situation to determine its appropriateness.

INFORMAL

FORMAL

If you had a vertical continuum and labeled the top "informal" and the bottom "formal" you could do the same thing. That is, think of people you know who are demonstrative in their facial expressions, are apt to hug you spontaneously and laugh easily, wear bright colors or different styles, even are sometimes radical. These you would place at the very top next to "informal."

Those acquaintances of yours who are more traditional, wouldn't think of wearing something that doesn't match and stand back a few feet when conversing with you, you might place on the bottom or the "formal" end. And then others who are a little this way and a little that way you would place somewhere in between.

In this exercise you are identifying the **POSTURE DIMENSION** of the people you know. Again, it's neither good nor bad, it is simply how they are; the appropriateness depends on the situation.

Four Behavioral Profiles

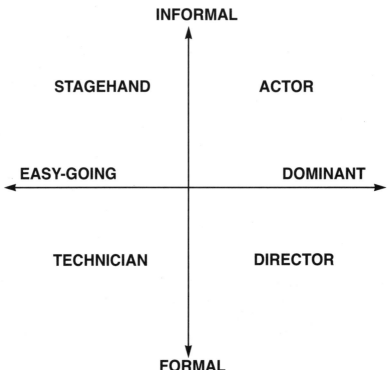

INFORMAL

STAGEHAND   ACTOR

EASY-GOING   DOMINANT

TECHNICIAN   DIRECTOR

FORMAL

    Now put those two dimensions together and you have four quadrants. Each represents a profile, a type of behavior, with dimensions of *ASSERTIVENESS* and *POSTURE*. For example, the upper-right profile is someone who is expressive, very relaxed and informal, makes quick decisions, likes to be on stage. I call this profile the *ACTOR*.

    The bottom-right is one who is decisive, driven, controlling, cool, calm and collected. They don't need to be on stage but they do prefer to call the shots. I call this the *DIRECTOR*. Both the *ACTOR* and the *DIRECTOR* profiles are challenging and outspoken. They will get the job done quickly but are very different in their methods and style.

    The bottom-left profile is one that exhibits caution, is detail-oriented, careful, slow to make decisions. Body movement tends to be limited and controlled, analytic in nature. I call this profile the *TECHNICIAN*.

The upper-left profile is friendly and warm, laid back and comfortable to be around. This profile is willing to take a supportive role, gets the job done from behind the scenes. I call this profile the *STAGEHAND.* Both the *TECHNICIAN* and the *STAGEHAND* are supportive but they are very different in the way they provide that assistance and communicate.

None of these styles is better than any other. Each has its own qualities and its own problems in interacting with others. *DIRECTORS* and *TECHNICIANS* are task-oriented, so it is essential to getting the job done well and on time. But they sometimes overlook people needs while *ACTORS* and *STAGEHANDS* are excellent at building and maintaining relationships but can be negligent in performing a task in a timely and thorough manner.

See how many people you can recognize in this brief list of "best" and "worst" of each profile. Most importantly, can you pick out your own dominant profile?

The Best and Worst of Each of the Four Behaviors

The Director can be at:

Best	Worst
A leader	Autocratic
Assertive	Demanding of self and others
Task-oriented	Unreasonable
Goal-oriented	Overbearing
Focused	Insensitive
Direct in language	Quick to judge
Decisive	Domineering
Efficient	Pushy
Time-disciplined	Severe
Rational decision maker	Harsh

The Technician can be at:

Best	Worst
Industrious	Uncommunicative
Persistent	Indecisive
Serious	Unyielding
Vigilant	Stuffy
Orderly	Exacting
Dependable	Impersonal
Calm	Unassertive
Moderate	Isolated
Casual	Withdrawn
Unaffected	Inexpressive

The Stagehand can be at:

Best	Worst
Supportive	Conforming
Respectful	Retiring
Willing	Noncommittal
Dependable	Undisciplined
Personable	Overly emotional
Contented	Nonassertive
Dependable	Affected
Assuring	Complaining instead of doing
Nonchalant	Needy
Lenient	Reactive

The Actor can be at:

Best	Worst
Personable	Opinionated
Stimulating	Excitable
Enthusiastic	Undisciplined
Dramatic	Reacting
Inspiring	Insincere
Creative	Confusing in directions
Assertive	Dominating in conversations
Fun	Ego-driven
Exciting	Impatient
Empowering to others	Thoughtless

You will notice that some styles share traits with others. For example both *STAGEHANDS* and *ACTORS* have traits that are relationship oriented. Both *TECHNICIANS* and *DIRECTORS* tend to be task oriented. But each is also unique. Did you see your friends', family's and coworkers' behaviors? Did you identify yours? Success on and off the job is determined by your ability to adapt and interact with each of them.

Getting Along with Them All

Success in dealing with each behavior is easy. You need only master two skills:

1. Be able to recognize each behavior

2. Develop assertive communication techniques that work with each behavior

You can learn to do both right now. The following is a look at four areas of verbal and nonverbal interaction.

> *Success is being able to recognize and*
>
> *Communicate with each behavioral style.*

Behavioral Clues Matrix

Behavior	Body Movements	Language Choice	Decisions	Facial Expressions
DIRECTOR	deliberate	precise	deliberate	controlled
TECHNICIAN	limited	exact	cautious	calm
STAGEHAND	flowing	personal	tentative	open
ACTOR	expressive	passionate	quick	animated

Tips for Asserting Yourself and Interacting with Directors

DIRECTORS move deliberately as if they know where they are going — most often they do! They use the correct words for the occasion and expect others to come to the point. They use language that is directive and may even sound sharp and demanding: "Do this now," "That isn't what I asked for," "Why did you do that," "What are the consequences?"

They need little information to make a decision. They are in control of their facial expressions, appear in control of themselves and want to control the situation, including you, if they think it will get the job done.

The assertive challenge with the *DIRECTORS* in your life is often to balance their need for control with your need to assert yourself. Here's how to do it!

If you work for a *DIRECTOR:*

- Be on time

    If you have a meeting, leave lots of time for unexpected delays. He or she will be on time and expect you to do the same.

- Communicate efficiently

    Limit personal conversations to polite inquiries. If you are unavoidably late, a quick precise explanation is sufficient, then get down to business. "There was an accident on 495 and traffic was diverted to the bridge. That's why I'm late. Shall we begin?" Use precise words to describe meaning.

- Be prepared

   Come with facts and figures. Be able to present the high points without excessive and unrelated personal opinions.

- Ask for what you want

   DIRECTORS respect and appreciate those employees who speak up and ask for what they need to do the job. If you don't get it, don't whine. *DIRECTORS* dislike and ignore whiners and complainers.

If *DIRECTORS* work for you:

- Give them responsibility

   You can delegate lots of tasks to your *DIRECTOR* employees, but you must also give them the authority to go with it. Check in from time to time but don't look over their shoulder. They will resent that and their performance will suffer.

- Let them be in charge

   They are good at running meetings, making decisions when you don't need a great deal of consensus, initiating action and overseeing follow-through. "Take charge of this meeting, Anne, and follow through on the implementation. Keep me informed." That kind of language gets *DIRECTORS* moving and happy. If they do not officially have some of those responsibilities as part of their job, they will do it anyway but may be resented by others and cause dissension on the team.

- Give specific directions

  If you want them to meet you at four o'clock, say so — not "around four." Give them exact directions on tasks. If you are the type who rambles when you give instructions, write them down for the **DIRECTORS** on your team.

If you have coworkers or personal relationships with **DIRECTORS:**

- Let them take the lead

  Whenever you can, let them take the lead in decision making and in conversations. If you can't or don't choose to, tell them. "I want to make this decision, John, because it affects me. So let me finish and then I will welcome your input." **DIRECTORS** love that kind of straightforward communication.

- Take care in passing judgment on their feelings

  Ordinarily **DIRECTORS** don't show a great deal of passion or excitement. But that doesn't mean they are not feeling excited or pleased or sad. When in doubt, ask, "Carol, you seem to be neutral on this issue. Is that true or am I misreading your reaction?" Remember, this style is direct and usually appreciates others to be direct as well.

Tips for Asserting Yourself and Interacting with Technicians

TECHNICIANS control and limit their body movements and facial expressions. They may even appear lethargic but that can be deceiving since you are observing behavior not intent.

As with **DIRECTORS** they use exact language but their word choice may be more precise and even less abundant. They may give one-, two- or three-word answers when you had hoped for more, "It should," "It was okay," "I don't know."

They are careful with decisions. Making sure they have every "t" crossed and every "i" dotted before moving forward.

The assertive challenge with the *TECHNICIAN* is often getting them to speak up and share thoughts, feelings and ideas. Here's how to do it!

If you work for a *TECHNICIAN:*

- Give lots of information

   Whatever your *TECHNICIAN* boss asks for in the way of information, give more. But make sure it is facts not fiction and that it is accurate. He or she will review all of it and, you can be sure, find an error if there is one!

- Listen carefully

   Since this style uses little language, you must listen to every word. Usually each word is important and there won't be a lot of additional and explanatory words to follow. If you don't understand, be sure to ask but you must ask for precisely what you want to know. "Rhonda, I need you to explain how the BOSE system works during a temporary power failure. That is, what information will it save and not save in that event?" *TECHNICIANS* rarely offer you more than you ask for.

- Take initiative

   Since this style is easy-going, sometimes you will need to step in and take action. Be careful in your tone and attitude, however. *TECHNICIANS* resent what they perceive as "pushy" behavior. "Steve, this parcel of land has not been advertised for six months. May I write and place an ad in this Sunday's classified?"

If a *TECHNICIAN* works for you:

- Give lots of information

   When assigning a task give as much information as you possibly can on how, why, when, and where. Then ask if the data is okay, "Ed, is there any additional information you might need? Have I covered everything?" This will save a great deal of your time later as the **TECHNICIAN'S** need to gather all the facts starts to unfold.

- Be patient

  TECHNICIANS are wonderful detail people so be patient. It will pay off in thorough work and solid follow-thorough although you may have to give a few nudges to start and restart most **TECHNICIAN** types.

- Assign work that is solitary and detailed

  This style usually works very well alone and is great on the details that other styles shun. When you have a one-person task or one that will take some painstaking concentration give it to your **TECHNICIANS**. You'll be happy with the results and they will be happy doing work that suits their style.

If you have coworkers or personal relationships with **TECHNICIANS:**

- Leave them alone

  Don't interrupt them any more than is necessary. They love their quiet time and will respond better to you if they have lots of time to themselves. When you must get their attention do so gently and be brief, "Norma, I know you're busy but this is important. What time does Gerry need to be at the gym today?"

- Ask them for information

  Since **TECHNICIANS** love to gather information, they end up with a great deal of it. You can rely on them to have the little details and an abundance of facts that others may find tedious or unimportant. "Harold, you worked on the Bresnahan account. What are the dimensions of their compartment for large equipment storage?" Be prepared for more detail than you may ever need or want!

- Be careful about interpreting their feelings

  As with **DIRECTORS**, **TECHNICIANS** do not always show what they feel. They can be absolutely ecstatic and yet exhibit a "poker" face and calm demeanor. Again, it doesn't mean they are unfeeling — behavior can be a poor measure of true passion with this behavioral style. Although **TECHNICIANS** can be evasive and noncommittal, you can get them to commit by giving them the reason for your interest and asking them a direct question. "Larry, it's important to me to know your feelings about this project. What is your reaction?"

Tips for Asserting Yourself and Interacting with Stagehands

STAGEHANDS make flowing gestures with their hands and body. Their faces are an open window, usually making it easy to guess their mood. They like to talk about themselves and love to know things about you. They use tentative language like, "Maybe," "Perhaps," "I think," "It should be," "It might have."

Decisions are considered well beforehand and they appear not to like to make yes-no, black-white, is-is not kinds of judgments, preferring instead to stay in the gray areas of "possibly" and "it might."

The assertive challenge here is getting **STAGEHANDS** to take a stand and take control when they don't wish to. Here's how to do it!

If you work for a **STAGEHAND:**

- Get to know him

  As far as you are able, and if it is appropriate, be on personal terms with your **STAGEHAND** boss. Before launching into a meeting or long conversation ask one or two personal questions.

  "How was your weekend, Fred? Did you get to play much golf?" As long as you are appropriate with content and timing, this friendliness will be noted and appreciated.

- Open up

  Again, as far as you are able and if it is appropriate, open up with personal information about you. Especially tell the **STAGEHAND** boss how you feel about your work, your opinions on the important matters of your work.

- Listen

  Of all the styles we will discuss, this one loves to be listened to. For example, if you go in for a performance evaluation, be prepared for a long session and listen intently. The **STAGEHAND** uses lots of words to describe feelings. You must listen to all of them to get the full content and flavor of the message.

If **STAGEHANDS** work for you:

- Give them tasks that are team-oriented

  They are strong team players. They will keep relationships flowing and soothe over rough spots when they occur. They like working with others and are good at it. If left to isolated tasks they will seek to socialize with others and production may suffer.

- Provide lots of follow-through and feedback

  Let them know how they are doing on a regular basis. They need to know they are appreciated and of all the behavioral styles respond particularly well to praise. "You're doing a great job on this report, Patty" can go a long way with a **STAGEHAND.** Check on their work more regularly than other styles, not because they are not good workers, but because they are often diverse in their thinking and get off track.

- Ask for their feelings and opinions

  They are motivated by feelings not facts. They will be more comprehensive about the precise data you might need from them if you ask their opinion from time to time. "Bob, I need the complete list of demographics on this community today. It would also help if you gave me your interpretation of how that might influence the marketing program we're launching there."

If you have coworkers or personal relationships with *STAGEHANDS*:

- Contact them frequently

  Most often you don't need to worry about interrupting or being too wordy with *STAGEHANDS*. They like frequent contact and warm, friendly open dialogue. They are usually the first to suggest social activities.

- Pay attention

  STAGEHANDS often talk a great deal and they want listeners. Don't let your mind wander if they are speaking to you. If it does happen, apologize sincerely right away. "I'm sorry, Jennifer, I was thinking of something else and didn't hear the last point you made." They are also quick to forgive and move on.

Tips for Asserting Yourself and Interacting with Actors

ACTORS love an audience and they respond with expressive and animated looks and movements. They show their passion and are quick to move, to take action. They are fun, great initiators and easily take leadership roles.

Their language is as passionate as they are. They use feeling words, exaggerate and are descriptive in their vocabulary choices, "I would just love to go with you. I have wanted to do that for a hundred years. What a stupendous idea." Sometimes they make up words when they can't find the right one. "That's a humungous pile of work you got there."

The assertive challenge with *ACTORS* is to get them off stage, graciously, without hurting their feelings. To assert but not hurt. Here's how to do it!

If you work for an *ACTOR*:

- Enjoy the ride

  They often change their passions and their focus on a whim. What was hot yesterday, today is not. You might as well enjoy it and learn to drop one project and pick up another as they become re-centered.

- Be friendly but brief

  Say good morning, greet them in the hallways and say goodbye when you leave. Don't have long conversations with them. Say what you have to say with as much animation as you can muster, and as much as the point demands, and go away.

- Show passion for ideas

  Be excited about their projects, but be honest. *ACTORS* can take a hit if they believe it comes from the heart. And they can change course in a moment, if your thoughts really make sense to them.

If *ACTORS* work for you:

- Praise them

  They love to be recognized, never shying away from the spotlight. You can get awesome results from *ACTORS* by making their results known. The fear of broadcasting poor results will keep them on track where they may otherwise lose focus.

- Let them express individuality

  ACTORS can work as well alone as part of a team. But they must have a central role from time to time otherwise they may create attention for themselves in ways that don't serve the organization well.

- Give them multiple tasks

  This behavior is the most adept at multitasking. To counteract their tendency toward lack of focus, give them a variety of tasks to do at once. Then don't be concerned if they bounce back and forth. Make sure you give them strong and clear deadlines, however, since time discipline is not a strength.

If you have coworkers or personal relationships with *ACTORS:*

- Invite them to your parties

  ACTORS are skilled at getting people to join in, take action and have fun. They are stimulating to have around in social gatherings and will get the conversation going when nothing else seems to work.

- Take their exuberance seriously

  Often people make the mistake of thinking excitable *ACTORS* are insincere, phony. Big mistake! They actually are not any more or less passionate than any other style, they just show it in a big way. And they mean it.

- Don't be offended by absence of attention from them

  If they don't show up when expected, don't call often or forget important dates, don't take this as a lack of interest in you. They are easily distracted and probably genuinely forgot. However, don't let them continue. Speak up. "Gary, you forgot my birthday yesterday and I was disappointed." Most *ACTORS* will fall all over themselves with apologies — and remember next time.

Three Points on Assertion and Behaviors

There are three critical points to take away from this chapter.

1. No style is better than any other

Each has its unique strengths and areas to improve upon. Relative to your own behavior, the key is to work on staying out of the "worst" sides and enhance and develop the "best" sides of your behavior. With regard to others' behavior, use the tips to interact with each according to the unique need of that behavior and the demands of the situation.

2. **You are all those styles — and so is everybody else**

   Although we each have a dominant style, one that we are generally recognized by and that we consider as our own, we all have the potential and at least some of the characteristics of all four.

3. **Don't label people, recognize behavior**

   That is, since anyone can be any of those behaviors, it isn't useful or accurate to label someone as a *DIRECTOR* for example, and then respond as if that were the only possible behavior for that person. Instead, note the current behavior of the person you are dealing with and use the tips that apply to that behavior.

Keep these three points in mind and you will be able to assert yourself with anyone, anytime and in any situation.

Review and Reinforcement

Key Points in This Chapter

- People have four basic behavioral styles: *DIRECTOR*, *TECHNICIAN*, *STAGEHAND* and *ACTOR.*

- These styles are neither good nor bad, just different.

- To assert yourself with each you must:

    1. Recognize the style

    2. Communicate appropriately

- Everyone has a dominant style as well as characteristics of all the other three.

Skill Practice

Find Your Primary Style

1. Circle a number on the horizontal continuum that best describes you. The higher the number, the more "dominant;" the lower the number, the more "easy-going." Remember, these words are to be taken as descriptive, not judgmental; that is, it is not good or bad to be either, it is simply a description of your style.

2. Circle a number on the vertical continuum that best describes you. The higher the number, the more "informal;" the lower the number, the more "formal." Remember, these words are to be taken as descriptive, not judgmental; that is, it is not good or bad to be either, it is simply a description of your style.

```
                        1
                        2
                        3
                        4
 1    2    3    4    5  | 6    7    8    9    10
                        6
                        7
                        8
                        9
                       10
```

Reflections

3. Draw two straight lines to find the intersecting point. (Note the example.) Relate the quadrant where your lines intersect to the corresponding behavioral style. That is, upper-right is *ACTOR*, lower-right is *DIRECTOR*, lower-left is *TECHNICIAN* and upper-left is *STAGEHAND*. This is your primary style.

STAGEHAND   *ACTOR*

1
2
3
4

1   2   3   4   5   6   7   8   9   10

6
7
8
9
10

TECHNICIAN   *DIRECTOR*

Reflections

Keeper Korner

Write down the most important point you learned or relearned in this chapter:

_____

_____

_____

4 TAKING ASSERTIVE ACTION AND GETTING RESULTS

"Thinking will not overcome fear, but action will."

— W. Clement Stone

All the knowledge in the world, all the understanding of behavior and how it works will not change or influence you or others. To get the results you want you must take action — positive, assertive action.

This chapter will teach you what action you need to take by implementing the next five steps in your *12 Positive Action Steps for Taking Charge of Your Life*. When you have completed this chapter, you will be able to:

- Identify the number one fear that keeps you from taking action

- Implement the four steps to get outside your Comfort Zone Box

- Say no without fear or guilt

- Use the five-part assertive conversation to control and influence

- See how perspective determines results

- Know when to give and when to give up

Positive Action Step #4: Grow

Why don't you say what you think? Why is it easier to think of what you should have said but not so easy to actually say it? Why is it sometimes so hard to say no? You probably can come up with many answers: fear of rejection, confrontation, failure, losing face, losing friends, and losing your job, to name a few. But all those reasons can be lumped into one word.

The Number One Enemy of Assertive Behavior

I have given a name to the most lethal enemy of assertive behavior. This name is the most important word in the world for those who wish to develop high-functioning behavior to handle negative people and situations. It is a word you need to memorize, keep in mind at all times.

This word is your assertive behavior enemy because it stops you — if you let it — from being assertive when you most need to be. It keeps you inside your Comfort Zone Box, prevents you from taking risk, from growing, from creating the life you can and should have.

Comfort Zone Box

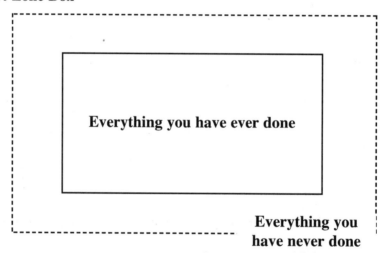

Everything you have ever done

Everything you have never done

But you can conquer this enemy — without losing anything and without adding unnecessary stress or anxiety to your life. Because you have all the tools you need to vanquish, to totally eliminate that enemy right now. First the word. The number one enemy of assertive behavior is *FUD*. That's right F-U-D — FUD!

FUD is your assertive enemy.

FUD creates your anxiety about what you "should have" said. FUD prevents you from saying "no" and then causes you stress later because you took on too much. FUD keeps you from getting the respect you deserve and limits the personal excellence and self-worth that you could enjoy in your life. What does FUD stand for? *FEAR*, *UNCERTAINTY* and *DOUBT*.

When you resist a healthy and assertive response to a person or situation, it's because you are afraid of reprisal, getting hurt, or hurting others. You are uncertain as to what the results will be and unsure if the reward balances the risk. You have doubt that you can handle the situation appropriately, intelligently and with strength and conviction. For these reasons, you stay inside your Comfort Zone Box, limit your growth and never learn or develop the assertiveness skills that could get you the life results you want. You don't have to stay there. There is a four-step process that will conquer FUD, get you out of the "box" and prepare you to take assertive action with anyone in any situation — and be successful.

Conquer FUD: A Four-Step Process

These four steps are available for anyone. Those who know what to say and when to say it, who suffer little guilt yet remain sensitive and understanding to others have mastered the four steps. So can you.

1. Build your knowledge

Only 10 percent of all professionals read nonfiction books, only 10 percent of all professionals go to seminars. If you are to take a leadership role in your life, be a role model for others, truly take charge of your life, you need to constantly increase your knowledge.

We have grown more in the past 50 years than we have since the beginning of humankind; we are growing exponentially. Our children will work for companies no one has thought of yet, they will build products and deliver services that haven't been invented. We've been to the moon, now we're going to Mars! And there are still some people walking around wondering if they should get a computer! What are they waiting for? To compete in this incredibly fast-paced and exciting world, you need daily infusions of knowledge.

2. Take action

The person who said, "Knowledge is power," was wrong. Knowledge is not power, the use of knowledge is power. You need to take action on the knowledge you acquire. And that action must change if it's not getting you the results you want. To continue to do the same thing and expect different results is insane.

Do something every day that will move you toward your goal. No matter how small, how inconsequential it might seem at the time, one action every day toward your goal will inspire you, move you forward and give you strength to act assertively when you need to.

3. Risk

Ordinary action isn't enough. You get out of bed every morning. That's an action. Will that by itself prepare you for the challenges and opportunities in your life? Of course not! You need to take risks. Do things you've never done before. Try out new ways. Get outside the "box"! How often do you say, "I can't do that." How do you know? Did you ask? When? Who? Did you try new ways to ask and approach different people? "I don't have the authority to make that decision," "I'm not sure that will be approved," "I've never done it that way." So what. Truly assertive people know that it's easier to get forgiveness than permission. That doesn't mean you take weird and wacky risks; that's dangerous.

Balance risk with knowledge, otherwise you take the biggest risk of all — a life of mediocrity. Our lives, our organization, our world cannot thrive on mediocrity. They may survive, limp along year after year, but they will not thrive.

> *Risk without knowledge is dangerous,*
>
> *Knowledge without action is a waste of time,*
>
> *But action without risk perpetuates mediocrity.*

4. Do it now!

How often do you say, "I'll think about it," "I'll do it later," "Tomorrow"? And then "tomorrow" becomes another "tomorrow" and yet another, and the action is never taken, the result never realized. Do things now. Don't put it off. Don't wait for more time, more money, more motivation. If you wait to do everything until you feel like it, you will miss half your life and half the excellence to which you are entitled. Take action. Do it now!

Positive Action Step #5: Take Action

You never need to walk away from a situation again and say, "I should have said." What follows is a Five-Part Assertive Conversation Model that, once learned, can be adapted to use in any confrontational situation you encounter.

The Goal

Before you even begin to prepare a conversation, you need to decide what you want to happen.

In other words, determine the results you want as a consequence of this encounter.

1. Select a situation

To make it real for you, think of something you want. Big or little, personal or professional, it doesn't matter. Perhaps you would like to make more money, have a bigger house, get a family member or roommate to participate more in cleaning up. Perhaps you want one of your staff members to come in on time or a coworker to stop annoying you. Think of something right now.

2. Identify the person

Next, who do you need to talk to to reach your goal or at least start the process. Your boss? Your husband, wife, significant other, roommate, child? A banker, a neighbor, a teammate? Who is the one person you need to speak to in order to get what you just said you want. Don't choose someone because you know they will agree with you. Choose the one person who has the authority, power or ability to give you what you want or to change what you wish changed.

3. Set your goal

What do you want out of this conversation? An agreement, a meeting, a promise for change? An apology, a report, a date? Make sure your goal satisfies three criteria:

Realistic

Is it possible for this person to accomplish your goal during or at the end of this conversation? For example, if you want to make more money, instead of "I want to double my salary in five years," a more realistic goal might be, "I want Terry to agree to a raise," or "I want Terry to agree to go to HR on my behalf and ask for a raise."

Specific

The more exact you are in what you want, the greater your chances of getting it. If you want your teenage son to come home on time, instead of "I want Andrew to be more prompt," you might say, "My goal is to get Andrew to agree to come home by 10:00 p.m. on weekdays and at midnight on weekends, and to call if he's delayed."

Clear

Make sure you know exactly what you want because if you don't, the other person surely won't. Instead of "I'm not happy with Evelyn's behavior," say "I want Evelyn to voice her complaints to me in private and offer positive alternatives."

Write your goal down in the margin of this page or somewhere you can see it as we go through the conversation model. Make sure it follows the rules of effective goals: that it is realistic, specific and clear.

> *Conversational goals must be*
>
> *Realistic, specific and clear.*

The Five-Part Assertive Conversation Model

For each part of this model, I will give you the *Content*, that is, what is contained in this step; a *Transitional Phrase*, that is, how you verbally get into this step; and *Examples*, that is, examples of how the step might be spoken in various situations.

As you read consider the situation, person and goal you just determined above. Think of how you would phrase each step with your own example using the five steps as your model.

1. Unacceptable Behavior or Situation

Content

Describe here what is not working or is unacceptable to you. Make sure you avoid inflammatory words and accusatory language. Phrases like, "You are ..." or "You never ..." or "Everyone agrees ..." or "I always ..." will immediately ignite anger and resistance. As a result the rest of your conversation will be unheard while the other person is mentally refuting your statement.

Transitional Phrase: "Here's what I have observed ..."

This doesn't accuse or blame; nor does it pass judgment. It simply notes observable conditions or behaviors.

Examples:

"Terry, here's what I have observed. Over the past year my responsibilities have increased but my income has not. Isn't that true?"

"Andrew, here's what I have observed. In the past two weeks, you have come home after 10:00 p.m. three times during the week and didn't call to say you were delayed. Would you agree?"

"Evelyn, here's what I have observed. At yesterday's team meeting when the new marketing plan was introduced you announced that you didn't like it and didn't want to implement it. Am I correct?"

Notice that the other person's agreement is requested. This is essential. To be successful at gaining that agreement, however, you must first present observable behavior or known conditions. For instance, if Evelyn was told, "You are always so negative" and then asked for her agreement, chances are slim that she would agree. Or if Andrew heard, "You're always late," or Terry was informed, "I have too much to do," it would be difficult to get their agreement.

If you make your descriptions objective and observable, not judgmental, most often the other person will agree, perhaps reluctantly, but agree none the less.

2. Your Reaction

Content

Tell the other person how you feel or what your reaction is to the behavior or conditions you described in Step 1. Be open and honest.

The more vulnerable you are willing to be now, the greater your influence will be later. That's because phrases like "I am" open doors. A sure-fire, shut-down phrase is, "You are not ..." Tell them you are angry or upset, frustrated or confused, but don't blame them for your feelings. "You make me ..." is the most dependable shut-down phrase you can use.

Transitional Phrase: "I feel ..." or "My reaction to this is ..."

No one can argue with how you feel or your reaction. With this kind of language you keep the door open and continue to invite dialogue.

Some people find it difficult using the word "feel," especially in a business environment, so I have offered the "reaction" phrase alternative. I suggest, however, that "feel" is a more powerful word and if you can use it comfortably, do so.

Examples:

"I feel pleased that you are willing to entrust me with more responsibility, Terry, but disappointed that my income has not kept current with my duties."

"When you come home at those times I feel disappointed. I am also concerned that you and I may not be clear on expectations. And, of course, I am always, and most of all, concerned about your safety when I don't hear from you."

"My reaction to your announcement was anger. This kind of response in front of the team can be demoralizing to the group and can set a negative tone for the whole implementation process."

3. Desirable Behavior or Condition

Content

This is where you tell the other person what behaviors or what changes you want to see. Have clear, well thought-out suggestions, with alternatives for this step. This step should be consistent with your goal. For instance, if your goal is to get someone to change their behavior, be sure you know what behavior you do want and even some alternatives if the first suggestion is rejected.

For example, if Andrew resists the 10:00 p.m. weekday curfew, you may want to have a backup. Like whenever he completes "x" amount of study above and beyond required homework he can add a half hour to his curfew. So first, have a definite plan to replace old behaviors and second, have a backup in case that he doesn't make it. So rule number one is be clear and concise with your suggestion; rule number two is have alternatives ready.

Transitional Phrase: "Here's what I think is fair ..."

Notice this phrase does not compel. It presents, it leaves room for dialogue, for discussion. If you are organizationally or otherwise subordinate to the other person, it is respectful. If you are the parent or the boss, you have built-in authority. In that case, using a phrase like this is gracious as well as open and inviting.

Examples:

"Here's what I think is fair. I would like you to look over this new job description I have written and then meet to discuss your reaction and, if you think it accurately reflects my current tasks, what compensation is appropriate."

"Here's what I think is fair. I suggest that if you find you can't make it home by 10:00 o'clock on week nights or midnight on weekends you call home at least 30 minutes before that time."

"Here's what I think is fair. When you disagree with a new promotion or project, you can announce that you have concerns and present them objectively or meet privately with me so we can work them out together before we involve the team."

4. Benefits

Content

This is where you tell other people how they will gain or what they stand to get by following your suggestions. This is the most important part of the conversation model. Unfortunately it is a part rarely included! Most people, even assertive people, will tell others what they don't like, what they want, and even get a commitment, but neglect to tell the other what's in it for them.

People have certain behaviors or encourage existing conditions because they believe they are getting something out of it. Until you show them they have more to gain by changing than by not changing, they will not change. They may try, may even sustain the new behavior or conditions for a short period of time, but to have long-term influence on others you must present them with believable advantages they can get if they are willing to do things as you suggest.

Transitional Phrase: "If you do this, it will …" or "I will …"

This phrase is not necessarily a trade-off, "If you do this, I'll do that," although it can be. Much more important, it is a delineation of the benefits possible to the other person.

Examples:

"If you do this, I can be more productive, knowing that I am appreciated in tangible ways for my additional efforts. My productivity will, of course, reflect on the whole department and you personally. Also, with official recognition in the organization, I won't have to come to you to mediate with other departments. That will be a time saver for you. You can spend more time on the other urgent tasks that only you can do. Those are attractive benefits to you, aren't they, Terry?"

"If you do this, I won't need to constantly remind you that you're breaking the rules. There will be less tension for us both and I think I would be more willing to give special favors when you're keeping the rules. Wouldn't that be better for you, Andrew?"

"If you do this, you will be more respected by your teammates. I can reflect that on your performance evaluation, which will give you greater growth potential in the organization. I know those things are important to you, Evelyn. Aren't they?"

Notice that in each case I asked the other person for concurrence that what I outlined as benefits were thought of as benefits by them as well. This is crucial. Not only are you continuing to engage the other person to keep this an open dialog rather than a speech, but you are requiring real consideration of the advantages. Remember, the only way people will change is if people see a greater advantage in doing so.

If you are at a loss as to what other people want, ask. Then try to negotiate a way for them to get that by giving you what you need.

5. Commitment

Content

Now you ask for a commitment. It must be a question that, if answered, will give you a yes or no to your suggestion. Don't ever assume due to body movement, facial expressions or general language that you have agreement or don't have agreement. Unless the person clearly verbalizes his or her reaction you have not brought the conversation to a conclusion.

This becomes critical in the follow-up stage. A great deal of the success of this conversation will depend on your follow-through and without this clear, positive statement of agreement you are in a weak position. A very common response from people after a conversation like this is, "Oh, I didn't know you wanted that ..." or simply "I agreed to nothing!" That's a frustrating position for the person attempting to change and influence. It won't happen to you if you get a clear commitment here, or at least find out now that you need to do something different to get that commitment.

Transitional Phrase: "When can I expect …?" or "When will this …?"

Notice that this phrase is a question and that it does not require a yes or no response. The latter can make agreement easier for the other person. While this phrasing implies you expect a definite and observable change, it does give some leeway as to when.

Examples:

"Terry, when will you be ready to discuss this new job description with me?"

"Andrew, when would you like to implement this new plan on curfew?"

"Evelyn, when would you like to meet to discuss your concerns regarding the new marketing program?"

Throughout this model conversation, notice that the other person was invited to participate in three places. Although they can speak, and often will, at any point, make sure that you engage your partners in at least three places:

Step 2: Gain concurrence on existing conditions or an observable action

Step 4: Ask if they want the advantages you suggest; if not, ask them what they do want

Step 5: Request a commitment to change; if they refuse, renegotiate

Use these transitional phrases until you know them by heart, until you are completely comfortable using them. Then, if you want to develop new ones for your unique situations, do so. Just be sure that the purpose and guidelines for each step are followed.

This conversation is a model. And as a model it can be adapted to any situation with any person. None of these examples or transitional phrases are cast in concrete, nor are they the only way to have an assertive conversation. But the concepts they represent are well-thought-out, historically successful ways to take charge, take action and get what you want.

Positive Action Step #6: Anticipate

The whole reason for developing a model and for planning out your conversation is so that you can anticipate. Often you don't respond assertively because you haven't time to think of what your reaction is, or haven't sorted out your thoughts and feelings. For all important encounters: Anticipate. Here is a three-part method to follow when you are planning a conversational encounter.

1. **Write out your side of the conversation**

   Using the model, consider what you will say and how the other person is likely to respond. Write this down. You need not write every word, just bullet the important points.

2. **Read it over and practice by yourself**

   Envision the encounter, how you will feel. Try to consider what the other person is feeling and thinking as well.

3. **Practice out loud**

   If it's a really important situation, get someone to play the part of the other person to take their side and give you an opportunity to be spontaneous, to see how you will handle it in a rehearsal. If you can't get anyone to role play with you, tape record your side and play it back.

This anticipatory activity will give you a large pay-back. First you have an opportunity to think about possible reactions and unplanned occurrences. This means you will handle yourself better because you have already thought it through and come up with a reply.

Second, having rehearsed, you are more comfortable with the points you will make. You will appear, and will be, more comfortable. The more comfortable and self-assured you are, the more likely you are to get what you want.

And third, if you can find a partner, this person can give you feedback on how you sound and appear. This objective observation before the main event is invaluable.

Now what's likely to happen? There are at least three possibilities. One: it will work. The other person will say, "No problem, I'll do it," and your issue is resolved. Two: it won't work. You rehearse, follow the model, do everything right and you get blown away by the other person. They flatly refuse. Three: Their words are "yes" but their actions are "no." The other person agrees to everything but nothing changes.

I cannot predict if it will work for you, and in the way you want it, but I can tell you under what conditions it won't work and that is the following. If you right now are saying, "This isn't going to work. I know this person and she'll never change. It might look good on paper, in a book, but in reality it's not going to work for me." Guess what? You're right. It won't work.

Positive Action Step #7: Be Positive

More than anything else, your success or failure in your assertive encounters will depend on one and one thing alone — your perspective.

Case Study: Me First

Doug walks into his supervisor's office and says, "I want my project put ahead of everybody else's." His supervisor responds, "Well, Doug, if you go out and ask everyone else if it's okay with them and they agree, it's a deal."

What is Doug's supervisor, a villain or a hero?

If you said a hero, I agree. After all, she considered the whole team, not just Doug. She empowered Doug to find his own solutions. She delegated, a critical management tool.

If you said a villain, I also agree. Who's boss around here anyway? She's supposed to be making the decisions. After all, she should have a view of the larger picture, be providing leadership for all.

Do you see what we did? We built evidence to support two opposing views: she's a hero and she's a villain. We could do that because of one critical human factor. Because you have 100 percent control over your perspective. You can build evidence to support any perspective you want.

You can drive to work in the morning saying, "What a loser I am. I just can't stand up to my boss. Even if I do, he always shoots me down. Just yesterday I asked him for the Braintree account and he refused. I just can't be assertive." Or you can build other evidence, "I'm a very powerful person. I can say anything I want to my boss. As long as I'm respectful, the worst he can do is say no. After all I got the job in the first place, that took assertiveness. I'm going to try to get that Braintree account again. I'll try a new strategy this time."

If you're saying, "Why should I change my perspective? I like hating my boss, I get a lot of sympathy that way. If I didn't complain about him, what would I do until 10 o'clock each morning?" Good question. You want to make sure there's a bigger benefit if you change behavior, right? Okay, consider this.

Case Study: The Villain

Doug steps out of his supervisor's office totally depressed. "What a witch. She couldn't make a decision if her life depended on it. Now I have to ask everyone on the floor for permission. I just absolutely know they'll never agree. This is miserable. 'Oh Carl, I have to ask you something. Now I know you're going to say no but' …"

How far will Doug get with Carl? Not far, I would say. Now consider this.

Case Study: The Hero

Doug steps out of his supervisor's office totally thrilled. "What a great opportunity. She is one great leader. She made me boss over this issue. Now I get to show how well I can manage an important situation. And who better to present this than me; after all, I know my situation best. 'Oh Carl, I want to talk to you about something that's going to affect your projects and mine. Please sit down ...'"

In which case will Doug get better results with Carl? The second, of course. It's important to adjust perspective to the situation, because perspective drives attitude, attitude impacts behavior and behavior creates results. You want better results? Change your perspective. You have 100 percent control over it.

> *Perspective drives attitude,*
>
> *Attitude impacts behavior,*
>
> *Behavior creates results.*

You can build evidence to support any perspective you want. And that more than anything else will determine your success in your Five-Part Assertive Conversation, and in your life. It's your choice.

Now what about the second and third possibilities. You do everything right, you have a great attitude, and they say no or they say yes but nothing happens. In the latter case, to turn this around three conditions must exist. First, set an exact time when this new behavior or condition will change. Second, get a clear agreement on what will change. Three, address the situation immediately if it doesn't occur when and how you agreed.

For example, let's say boss Terry agrees to meet to discuss your new job description on Monday at 2:00 p.m. You show up, he's not there. You leave a note on his desk, "Did I misunderstand our agreement that we were to meet today at 2 o'clock?" As soon as you see him set a new date and follow through. The same with Andrew and Evelyn. The other person will get it that you mean it and in most cases with diligence and persistence ultimately you will succeed.

"But," you say, "what about when I do everything, even follow through and it still doesn't work. What then?"

Positive Action Step #8: Persist

Can you change anyone else? No. Can you influence others? Yes. Can you influence everyone? No. Know when your persistence is well placed and when it's not. Some people choose not to be influenced. Some are not ready. Some never will be. They are not bad, they are different, they are exercising their right of choice. Perhaps you need to move your efforts elsewhere. Use these guidelines to help you decide.

You cannot influence others when:

- They refuse to change.

   It is their right.

- There are situations outside theirs or your control.

   Spend your time on that which you can influence.

- You are dogmatic or insensitive.

   People respond to those who take the time to understand them.

- You are not fully committed.

   Decide your level of commitment first; you don't have to take on the world.

You can influence others when:

- They cooperate.

   Even if it's only a little, work with what you've got.

- You are realistic in your expectations.

  As long as they are trying, be patient and be positive.

- You are willing to be flexible about outcomes.

  Accept change even if it's a little different from what you expected or wanted.

- You are sensitive and aware of others' needs.

  The more you know about the needs of others, the more you can influence them and the more they will be willing to support you.

You can now have all your encounters — personal or professional — meet your expectations.

Review and Reinforcement

Key Points in This Chapter

- The number one enemy of assertive behavior is FUD.

- Conquering FUD requires knowledge, action, risk and doing it now!

- A clear goal is necessary before any important conversational goal.

- The Five-Part Assertive Conversation Model includes:

  1. Describing unacceptable behavior

  2. Expressing your feelings or reactions

  3. Presenting desired behavior or conditions

  4. Listing the advantages of change

  5. Asking for a commitment

- Follow-through, perspective and persistence commensurate with commitment will determine success.

Skill Practice

Take a professional or personal situation that you wish to create change and fill in the following:

Describe the behavior or conditions that are unacceptable:

Write the person's name who can change this:

Write down your conversational goal (be sure it is realistic, specific and clear):

Reflections

Using the Five-Part Assertive Conversation Model write out your side of the encounter:

1. "Here's what I observe ..."

2. "I feel ..." or "My reaction is ..."

3. "Here's what I think is fair ..."

4. "If you do this I will ..." or "It will ..."

5. "When can I expect ..." or "When will you ..."

Check here when you plan to have this conversation:

❑ I will have this conversation today

❑ I will have this conversation within two weeks

❑ I will have this conversation but I'm not sure when

Reflections

Keeper Korner

Write down the most important point you learned or relearned in this chapter.

_____

_____

_____

5 QUALITIES OF LEADERSHIP

"Whatever you focus your attention on will govern your life."

— Brian Tracy

Whether you are a manager, supervisor, team leader or team player, the head of your family or one of its members, you are a leader. You may lead others or take leadership of your own life but if you choose to live an assertive life you must have the qualities of leadership on and off the job. This chapter will give you all the tools to do that.

The primary qualities of leadership are contained in the next four steps to your *12 Positive Action Steps for Taking Charge of Your Life*. When you complete this chapter you will be able to:

- Recognize and adopt all the characteristics of leaders

- Avoid focusing on the minutiae

- Take charge of your five life areas

- Teach others to lead and assert themselves

- Use the Three Rs for personal and professional success

- Give effective feedback — and take it!

- Make and keep commitments

- Prevent the three most common commitment errors

- Appreciate fully your worth to yourself and others

Positive Action Step #9: Lighten Up

Did you ever notice that really good leaders, effective leaders, those who have long-term positive, impact on others most often have a happy and joyful attitude toward life? And yet they usually have the greatest burdens, are responsible for the most significant problems. I don't mean they are never sad or angry or frustrated, but I do mean that they seem to save those emotions for the really big issues, while they rise above the small daily inconveniences.

Focus on the Big Stuff

People follow those who can see the big picture. Leaders do not get bogged down in the minutiae, the irrelevant, the unimportant. They don't set themselves up to be dragged down by every little thing they don't like. They rise above, they lighten up.

I do hundreds of seminars every year and at the end of each one, I ask people to evaluate their experiences that day. Most people relate the extraordinary growth they have created for themselves. I am so touched and proud to be associated with so many uplifting individuals.

But there are occasional seminar attendees whose feedback on those evaluations would be amusing if it wasn't so sad. After spending an entire day exploring their own life possibilities, their summation of the day is something like, "The coffee ran out." I'm talking about their life and they're focused on coffee!

> *Focus on minutiae*
>
> *And that will drive your life.*
>
> *Focus on greatness*
>
> *And you will be part of that greatness.*

What have you been focusing on since you began reading this chapter? Answer these questions to help you focus throughout this book in ways that will help, not hinder your growth:

- What was I thinking about as I began reading this chapter?

- Will that thought help me or someone else in any way?

- In which of the following areas should I concentrate my efforts right now?

    — A specific personal or professional goal? Which one?

    — A specific individual who needs my support?

    — One problem or opportunity that could be improved by being more assertive? What is it?

    — My life in general? Being open to find ideas as I uncover them here?

    — Something else? What is that?

Don't be one of those looking for what you don't like, or what isn't working for you. Spend this precious reading time looking for ways you can use the information to enrich your life and the lives of others. Rise above. That's leadership, that's an assertive life.

Positive Action Step #10: Take Care of Me

Chronic complainers usually talk about that which they can't do anything about. Notice that those people who constantly whine and complain about the weather, upper-management decisions, organizational policies, governments, other departments, their neighbors, are those least likely to take action where they can: their own job, their health, family issues, etc.

I'm not talking about functional, productive conversations that explore solutions or inform, I'm talking about the moaners and groaners who have no purpose in their conversation except to complain. Assertive leaders find ways to work with those things they cannot change and change the things they can.

"Response - Ability"

"There is so much to remember and do to live an assertive life," people often say to me. "Is there one word or phrase that I can hold on to, that will give it all to me? One message to guide me through any circumstance." My answer is always, "Yes, there is!" I offer the word to you: ***RESPONSE-ABILITY***.

Stephen Covey in his magnificent work, *The 7 Habits of Highly Effective People,* said, "Response-ability is our 'ability' to 'respond.' What matters most in life is not what happens to us but how we respond to it."

Dr. Victor Frankl, in *Man's Search for Meaning*, said, "Everything can be taken from a man but one thing: the last of the human freedoms — to choose one's attitude in any given set of circumstances, to choose one's own way." Frankl was an Auschwitz survivor. He survived one of the worst events in human history and then said it was his choice! Not what happened to him, that was not his choice as many things in your life were not your choice — but how he responded, he said, was his choice. What an awesome role model.

Five Life Areas You Control

Consider the areas of your life that are troublesome to you right now. Can you do anything about any of them? If yes, do so. If not, develop ways to work within if you can but absolutely don't complain about them. Remember your response is your choice. Choosing to complain is not the attitude of a winner. A leader is a person living an assertive life.

> *You cannot control anything*
>
> *Until you take control of yourself.*

Developing the qualities of leadership means starting with the basics. And within those basics — those fundamentals of your life — you have a great deal of control. Here are five areas that you can enhance and improve at will. Take on the action plan that follows each. This will affect all other areas of your life.

Five Life Areas

1. Physical

You will need a great deal of energy to take charge of your life, to actualize yourself in your career, to be an effective role model to your friends and family. You have the power to affect that energy. What makes up your diet? You have complete control over what you eat. If your diet consists of large volumes of sugar, salt, fat and highly processed foods, then you are compromising your future success. Does that mean you can never have a hot fudge sundae? No, of course not. But it does mean you can't have six a week. If you take in huge quantities of caffeine and alcohol or if you smoke, you compromise your ability to meet future challenges successfully.

How much exercise do you get? Most experts agree that you need two hours a week of regular rigorous exercise. What about rest? You may have to miss some things or others may have to do without you from time to time so that you can get the rest you need. You are no good for yourself or anyone else unless you are rested.

Action: Write down your current health plan regarding diet, exercise and rest. Take it to an expert. After getting expert input, design a plan for health that will fit into your schedule as well as satisfy your health goals.

2. Emotional

Did you ever watch a soap opera? Did you ever notice that if you missed six months of episodes and then watched it again, the same things would be happening? The same villains would be up to their dastardly deeds and the same heroes would be saving the day. The actors' conversations would center on the same theme: who's doing what to whom.

What are you worried about right now? What do you want in your life that you don't have or have enough of? How long have you been concerned about that? A month? A year? Five years? Ten years? What are you waiting for? Don't be a walking soap opera.

Action: Find out who you have to talk to to get what you want. Call, write or visit them. Find out what you have to do and do whatever it takes. If there is risk involved, decide if the risk is worth it. If it is, do it. If it's not, don't do it. But then remove the worry from your list of wants and replace it with something where the risk is acceptable to you. That's taking control of your emotions, that's being assertive.

3. Intellectual

You have already seen the value and necessity of knowledge in your life. I meet many people who are not satisfied with their organizational growth. They often have degrees, some have graduate degrees. I ask them, "How long ago did you graduate?" They tell me two years ago, or five or ten. I then ask them, "What is your current intellectual pursuit?" After they "hmm" and "uhhh" for a while I see that the answer is really, "Nothing." These people are learning dropouts!

If you are not involved in a structured learning process right now — whether you designed it yourself or you are in some formal program like a college or university — you are a learning dropout. Do you need less money now than when you were in school? Do you have less responsibility? Fewer options? If you are like most people, you need, want and have more — need more money, have more responsibilities and want more options!

It is no longer possible to graduate from high school or college and clap your hands in glee saying, "Well that's done. Now I can live my life." You need, as you saw earlier, daily infusions of knowledge to be a success in this fast-paced, highly competitive, extraordinary, whirlwind world in which we live.

In Denis Waitley's *Psychology of Winning*, he notes that rich and powerful people always have libraries full of resources. "Do they have so many books because they're rich," he muses, "Or are they rich because they have so many books?"

Action: Decide on an amount of time today that you will devote to your lifelong learning and begin the process immediately. Build you own personal resource library.

4. Social

We are social beings. We need others to be fulfilled. And we need that contact to friendly, relaxing, fun. Neither be a workaholic nor a sociaholic. Balance your time between career and family and time just for you.

Take care in your selection of those with whom you socialize, especially personal contacts where you often have more control than professional contacts. Surround yourself with people who energize and validate you. I made a vow many years ago that I would not keep anyone in my life who took more joy out than they put in. That vow has required me to make some tough decisions over the years, and I have made exceptions from time to time, but I believe it has contributed greatly to my thorough enjoyment and excitement with my own life.

Don't let family members rob you of your joy just because they are family. Help them grow and become enlightened. And if they will not, you may have tough decisions to make. At least don't focus on their complaints. Tell them, "I'm committed to having a joyful, productive and assertive life. I would like to help you do that as well. But if you don't want to, it's your right. I will be exercising my right not to listen or be involved with anything that will prevent my growth."

Also, give yourself the gift of time alone. Some people need less alone time than others. But whatever your needs are, arrange your schedule so that you have at least some time to be with the person who will never leave you — you.

> *Learn to enjoy your own company.*
>
> *You are the one person who will never leave you.*

Action: Take on a new hobby. Something you can get passionate about — that will allow you to be with people of similar interests or that will give you time alone. Even if you can only afford 15 minutes a week to this project, it's a start. If it's something you truly enjoy and develop skill at it, you'll find more time.

5. Spirituality

To some people spirituality means religion, to others it's nature, or music or philosophy. Whatever it is to you when you go there — and it's not necessarily a physical place, it can be prayer, meditation, or just thinking quietly — you become grounded in your own values.

When you are grounded in your own value system, your priorities snap into position. When that happens, you can step out into the world and meet any challenge life can offer because that's your integral core. People of integrity have something that less integral people don't have. People of integrity have a freedom. A freedom that allows them to judge themselves, that allows them to center on respect instead of being liked.

Action: Go to your spiritual place, whatever or wherever that is for you. Get grounded in your own value system and when you are clear about your values, list your priorities. Stick to them. Focus your energies on them. As long as your values come from a good and honest place, your priorities will get you through all the rough spots.

Positive Action Step #11: Have Patience

Give Yourself Time and Opportunity to Grow

Dr. Martin Luther King, Jr. once said, "I may not be the man I could be, I may not be the man I ought to be, I may not be the man I can be but praise God, I'm not the man I used to be." It took years for you to become the wonderful person that you are and it will take time for you to improve and enhance that person. Be patient with yourself as you implement the 12 Positive Action Steps. Here are four ways to let yourself grow at a pace that is comfortable for you and that will get results as well.

Four Ways to Grow

1. Role model others

Notice people you admire and respect. See how they assert themselves verbally. How they move their bodies, especially how they walk. If you can, talk to them about their assertive behavior. Find out how they handle rejection and fear. Do they have any special techniques or quotes they use when they feel hurt or insulted? Everyone experiences these emotions but assertive people have learned to manage them more successfully.

Then do what they do. Start with just one or two things. It may feel uncomfortable at first but if you are committed and persist, ultimately this adjustment will become part of your own behavior.

2. Get feedback

Align yourself with someone you trust to offer you guidance and advice as you grow. Ask them how you appear at meetings. "Do I have any mannerisms that make me appear less powerful? For example, do I put my hand over my mouth when I talk? Do I avoid eye contact? Do I speak in volume or tone so that others must lean in to hear me?"

Ask about your dress and posture as well as your words and demeanor. It is essential that you trust this person. This must be someone who will tell you the truth but who won't unnecessarily hurt your feelings. Use this feedback as a way of adjusting and making changes as needed. Remember also that you are the best judge of your progress. Take the feedback, but use it as a guide not as a directive.

3. Teach others

To fully master this subject you must do three things: gather, adapt and teach.

a. Gather

Right now you are gathering the information you will need to tap into your assertive behavior.

b. Adapt

You have been given an abundance of action items, suggestions, methods, and tools to adapt and integrate into your professional and personal life. You will continue to get many more throughout this book.

c. Teach

There is no greater way to learn than to teach somebody else. Take every opportunity to tell others what you know. You will help them and develop a fuller understanding of the information yourself.

Give Others Time and Opportunity to Grow

Feedback seems to be one of the most difficult things to do. One of the primary things I do as a consultant is to teach people in organizations to give good effective feedback. Most people seem to handle their relationship problems by not speaking to one another, by being rude, by making sly remarks or gossiping behind the other person's back. None of these methods is effective. On the contrary, they can cause deeper damage that hurts feelings and delays productive work.

Teaching others will require that you have as much patience with their progress as with your own and that you give good effective feedback. Whether you are a manager and are required to give feedback to your staff, a parent offering guidance to your child or just someone who wants to be helpful to others, you will benefit from the teaching tool called, The Ethics of Effective Feedback. See the description of each and study a poor and good example of each.

The Ethics of Effective Feedback

To have long-term results and to be received well, feedback must be:

- **Vision-Driven**

    This means that the reason for your feedback is to further a team or family goal. It means that your purpose is not self-centered or manipulative.

    Poor example: "I'm going to show all the flaws in Harriet's proposal so that mine will be considered first" is a self-centered and manipulative reason for feedback. It is not vision-driven.

    Good example: "How can you adjust the implementation of your proposal, Harriet, to meet our time schedules?" is a vision-driven feedback statement.

- **Nonjudgmental**

  Feedback, to be effective, must be expressed in observations not value judgment. What you refer to must be an observable condition or situation not a comment on personality or attitude.

  Poor example: "You have a bad attitude, Al. You'd better shape up." This comment is likely to shut down all communication and is unlikely to get positive results.

  Good example: "You said at the meeting that the project is doomed to fail. That comment will set the program off to a poor start. We need your support. Tell us how to get you on board." Now Al has something concrete and positive to work on.

- **Specific**

  The other person must know exactly what behavior or condition is being addressed and what changes need to be made. Otherwise, even if the desire to improve is there, the knowledge of how is not.

  Poor example: "You handled that meeting poorly, George. You need to do better next time." George will decide what needs to be done better and the person giving the feedback may or may not get the desired results.

  Good example: "George, there was very little team involvement at your meeting. Next time I would like you to get input from each member during the meeting." Now George knows exactly what's expected of him.

- **Respectful**

  To be effective, the other person must leave you with the impression that your comments were based on behavior, not personality and that it is a specific behavior or condition, and that your remarks are for that person's improvement and/or the growth of the team or family.

Poor example: "I can't stand the way you look at me, Amy. You're always up to something sneaky." This is likely to drive Amy further into deceit if she is holding back or, if she's not, to become resentful.

Good example: "Amy, your look right now tells me there's something else I should know about this request. Please tell me so we can make the experience good for everyone." Now Amy has an open door and she hears a valid reason, "a good experience for everyone," to share anything she's held back.

Positive Action Step #12: Be Committed

It seems that for some people, keeping one's word is not as important as it used to be. Remember when you were a child and you actually believed it when someone told you something would happen? And you can probably still recall a time when you were promised something that you didn't get. You remember it many years later!

Someone calls and says, "I'll be over at three." They show up at quarter past and no one says anything. You tell a friend, "We'll have lunch next week." Next week comes and goes. No comment. I think commitments are more important than that.

You might say, "For goodness sake, you're talking about a meeting or a lunch date with a friend. Is that so important?" I don't know. But I do know this: I can't decide what is and isn't important to others. It will not work if I say, "Some commitments I'll keep and others I won't and I'll decide which those are."

> *Your word is your integrity.*
>
> *Your integrity is the rock*
>
> *Upon which assertiveness is built.*

If you still remember the thing that was promised to you as a child, it must have been really important to you. But someone else decided it wasn't. Is that fair? I think it's dangerous. It erodes integrity, the rock upon which assertiveness is built.

Three Common Commitment Errors

1. Minimizing

"It wasn't important anyway."

As you have seen once you make a commitment, only the other person can decide if it's important. Until that happens, all commitments you make are important.

"It was only a commitment to myself."

Perhaps the most important commitments you will ever make will be to yourself. After all, no one's opinion of you is more life-altering than yours.

2. Underestimating

"They probably forgot all about it."

Often people use this as an excuse, which really means, "I no longer want to do this." This is not only dangerous but usually inaccurate as well. Don't take a chance. Keep your promise or ask, but don't assume.

3. Fear of reprisal

"I'm embarrassed to face them."

Owning up to an inability to keep a commitment may be temporarily uncomfortable for you. But avoiding the person and breaking your commitment can erode that person's faith in you and cause you personal stress. Clearly that is a greater risk.

"They'll be angry."

Perhaps they will. That's the downside of having to renegotiate, but their anger is better than their mistrust of you. Most times you can rebuild a relationship with someone who is angry but mistrust is a more formidable break and harder to heal.

Maintaining Your Reputation of Integrity

Most things you have can be taken away or will be used up. But your word is you. No one can take that kind of integrity away. That's the kind that builds character. The kind that establishes a reputation, "When Paul makes a promise, you can depend on it." That's powerful, that's assertive, that's leadership. Assertive leaders make and keep commitments.

I have people say to me in seminars, "I never break a commitment. Because I never make a commitment unless I'm absolutely positive I can do it." What kind of a life is that? To never step out. To never commit without evidence. Never to take a chance, to risk and then put all your efforts and will to make it happen? I think that's an "inside the box" life! One that will never test strength or allow one to stretch.

"But," you may say, "what happens if I have every intention of keeping my word and something happens beyond my control. Or a more critical commitment overrides it?" Good question. Because those things do happen. Don't they? Here's the answer. There are three things you can do with a commitment: keep it, break it or renegotiate it.

When you keep your commitments

That usually works for everyone. Others trust you, see you as a serious person, assertive, one to whom they ought to pay attention.

When you break your commitments

That usually doesn't work for anyone. Few people take you seriously. They will find it easy to break their commitments to you. You will not be viewed as someone of power and worth. This may eventually impact how you think of yourself.

When you must renegotiate your commitments

That can work or not work. It depends. If you use it as a back door when you made the commitment, "If the going gets tough, I can always renegotiate," that attitude will be transparent and you will be no better off than the person who breaks commitments.

Use this option rarely and only if absolutely necessary. Go to the person to whom you made the commitment as soon as you know you can't keep it, giving reasonable honest evidence as to why you must renegotiate. Be as flexible as you can in your renegotiation — after all you are changing the agreement. If you do this, chances are good you will be treated as someone who keeps his commitments.

Example: "I know I promised you this report today. I have done everything I could to ensure that would happen. However, an hour ago I was asked by the company president to intercede on her behalf with a customer — a very large customer who is threatening to take business away. The situation is urgent and I am most in touch with the details. I need to renegotiate with you. I'll be as flexible as I can on a new date. What is the next best date you can give me?"

You now have all the tools you need to continue your development and to demonstrate the primary qualities of leadership.

Review and Reinforcement

Key Points in This Chapter

- If you choose to live an assertive life you must demonstrate the qualities of leadership on and off the job.

- Leaders:

    — rise above the minutiae and focus on the greater issues

    — take control first of those things they can control

    — allow themselves and others time and room to grow

    — make and keep commitments

- To master a subject you must: learn it, practice it, teach it to others.

- Three things you can do with a commitment are — keep it, break it, renegotiate it. All have consequences.

- The three most common commitment errors are: minimizing, underestimating, fear of reprisal. All have consequences.

Skill Practice

Leaders:	Others:
Make things happen	Wonder what happened
Give credit to their team	Worry about getting credit
Look for solutions	Place blame
Take initiative	Wait and see before acting
Are strong enough to be humble	Fear and resent humility
Develop their weak areas	Try to hide weaknesses
Practice their strengths	Show off their good points
Take pride in their accomplishments	Brag about their results
Correct mistakes	Make excuses for mistakes
Help others grow strong	Are jealous of others' strength
Take risks	Stay safe
Encourage change	Fight for the status quo
Forgive	Never forget
Identify fears and work to conquer them	Deny their fears
Present what could be	Talk about what was
Strive toward for excellence	Want to be perfect
Take charge when and where they can	Complain
Let go when they must	Hang on uselessly
Recognize the good	Look for faults

Reflections

Keeper Korner

Write down the most important point you learned or relearned in this chapter.

_____

_____

_____

6 12 POSITIVE ACTION STEPS: A SUMMARY

> *"The quality of a person's life is in direct proportion*
> *to their commitment to excellence,*
> *regardless of their chosen field of endeavor."*

— Vincent J. Lombardi

This chapter contains all 12 of the Positive Action Steps you have covered in this book.

For each step you will find a:

- Review of the most salient points regarding that step

- Red flag section, showing the danger signs, so you can judge where you most need improvement

- Tools for guidance so you can tap into your intrinsic assertive behavior, take charge of your life and influence others

- List of expectations; that is, the benefits you will receive as you develop expertise and strength in each step

Positive Action Step #1: Like Me

Review

Your self-esteem more than anything else will determine how successful you will be in tapping into your abundant supply of assertiveness. This is not a one-time accomplishment. A strong self-esteem will require vigilant repetition of certain behaviors. It is something others can see and hear from the outside in your language and body movements and you can feel from within in your willingness to speak up without guilt or fear. You have more to gain by developing a firm foundation here than in any other step and more to lose by ignoring its value to your assertive life.

Red Flags

You need work in this area if you:

- Frequently doubt if you said or did the right thing

- Minimize your worth or nullify compliments by saying, "I could never do that," "It was really nothing," "You shouldn't have done that, I don't deserve all this"

- Often avoid eye contact, walk with your head down, stand with your arms folded or with your hands in your pockets

- Dread being singled out for acknowledgment or reward

Tools for Guidance

These tools will make this positive action step strong and consistent in your life:

Tool 1: Do one thing just for you every day. It doesn't have to be a big thing or even take a great deal of time. But at least once a day do something that you like to do, that allows you to feel good or happy or at peace with yourself.

Tool 2: Monitor how you speak to and about yourself. Make your language that which you would use if referring or conversing with your best friend or a loved one.

Tool 3: Check your walk, hand movements and eye contact to ensure you are sending an assertive message to the world.

Expect ...

Using the above tools you can expect:

- A feeling of confidence about your actions and decisions

- An increase in the respect and trust given you by others

- More clarity and confidence in your descriptions and statements

- Lack of guilt, greater ability to cope with stress

Positive Action Step #2: Know Me

Review

There is no thing intrinsically bad or good about passive or aggressive behavior. There are times when you need to be passive — when learning or listening, etc. — and times when you should be aggressive — in an emergency or urgent situation. Assertiveness, therefore, cannot be found in the middle of the Passive-Aggressive Continuum. Assertiveness is choosing the right behavior for the situation. You can find that place unfailingly by using the Assertive Belief. That is by a balanced belief in your rights and the rights of others.

Red Flags

You need work in this area if you:

- Question why you didn't speak up or said too much after a confrontation

- Find that people frequently ask you to speak up or tone down your volume

- Believe that everybody else is just "lucky" or they are all "poor souls"

- Feel victimized or like pushing others around

Tools for Guidance

These tools will make this positive action step strong and consistent in your life:

Tool 1: Get a mentor, someone who will give you an honest evaluation on how you treat others, the pitch and volume of your voice, your fairness. This may not be easy. People rarely like to give honest evaluations of others. If you are seen as excessively aggressive, they may fear you. In this case, be sure to select someone over whom you have no authority, who has nothing to fear from you. If you are unnecessarily passive, they may not want to hurt your feelings. In that case, you must convince them that you want to grow and need their help.

Tool 2: When or if you feel victimized, list your rights in the situation.

Tool 3: If you suspect that you've taken advantage of someone, list their rights or ask them to do so.

Expect ...

Using the above tools you can expect:

- Better results in your interactions with others

- People to be more open and vulnerable in their behavior around you

- Good feeling about yourself and others — that feeling will be returned tenfold!

- To be more calm during interactions even when they are emotional

Positive Action Step #3: Know Them

Review

You live in a world of differences. Differences of behavior, needs, values and style give life its variety and mystery as well as its problems. The best way to deal with others successfully is to understand them, even if (or especially if) you don't like them. Some people are task-oriented and they can appear cold or uncaring. Others seem so focused on relationships it looks like the job will never get done. In reality, they are just expressing their dominant style, which has both strengths and areas for growth opportunity. Learning to deal with all of them can make a huge difference in your ability to assert yourself.

Red Flags

You need work in this area if you:

- Don't like a lot of people

- Avoid certain types of people because you can't get along with them

- Make sweeping behavior statements like, "I don't like loud and aggressive people" or "People who are _____ really turn me off"

- Give up easily or just talk louder and faster when you don't get your way

Tools for Guidance

These tools will make this positive action step strong and consistent in your life:

Tool 1: Make a list of your responsibilities on the job. Prioritize this list as A-B-C. That is, put an A next to those things that are most critical, B next to those things that are less critical, etc. Ask your supervisor or manager to list what he or she sees as your primary responsibilities. Then compare the lists. This will open dialogue and allow both of you to see if you have major differences and if so where they are.

Tool 2: Do the above with family members. This can do wonders for smoothing out household arguments as to who is supposed to do what and when.

Tool 3: Have everyone on your team look at the behavioral styles section here and pick out their style. Let each member list three things they would do differently when others deal with them and three things they will do or improve when dealing with everyone else. A great team exercise — at work or home!

Expect ...

Using the above tools you can expect:

- Your relationships to improve

- To handle touchy or sensitive issues with others better

- To like some people you thought you didn't

- More flexibility among team members

Positive Action Step #4: Grow

Review

Sometimes it seems overwhelming to manage the plethora of information and handle all the work that is required. But putting off what must be done loads you with unnecessary guilt and anxiety and detracts from your innate assertiveness. There is a formidable enemy that keeps you from growth and action and that enemy is FUD — Fear, Uncertainty and Doubt. FUD keeps you stagnant, doing what you've always done, safe — and bored — inside your Comfort Zone Box. But there are strong weapons to fight this enemy. These weapons are knowledge, action, risk and now.

Red Flags

You need work in this area if you:

- Are complaining about the same things today as you were last week or last year

- Have not achieved the success you thought you would at this stage of your life

- Can think of more reasons why you "shouldn't" than why you "should"

- Avoid change

- Don't feel actualized in your work or your relationships

Tools for Guidance

These tools will make this positive action step strong and consistent in your life:

Tool 1: Write down the significant problems that you are faced with right now and that you find yourself focused on a good deal of the time. Put this list in the bottom of a drawer and don't look at it again for three months. If you find you have the same issues in three months, either place an action plan next to each one or cross it off your list. You can have a working plan for a problem or you can dump it but you cannot keep it.

Tool 2: Write on a piece of paper, "My vision of how my life should be is ..." Complete that statement regarding four life areas: career, relationships, health and finances. Now develop strategies to bring your current reality up to your vision. It doesn't matter how long it takes for each one as long as you're working on them.

Expect ...

Using the above tools you can expect:

- Your life to become what you want instead of what others tell you it should be

- To be happy more

- To focus on improving the big things in your life instead of fretting about the details

- Things to happen when you didn't even seem to do anything except to think of what could be

Positive Action Step #5: Take Action

Review

Complaining will never change a situation, only action will. Have functional conversations with people to get what you want. To achieve your expectations you must make them known. You have a right not to let people annoy, disrespect, interrupt or stand in your way. But you must let them know first by using the *Five-Part Assertive Conversational Model*. First tell them what the unacceptable behavior or condition is, without blaming, without inflammatory language. Second, express your feelings or reaction to this situation — your feelings, no one else's. Third, present the changes you would like to see, clearly, concisely. Fourth, list the advantages to them if they agree to this plan. Fifth, ask for their commitment, make it specific and time-sensitive. Follow up immediately and with conviction to ensure that your agreement sticks.

Red Flags

You need work in this area if you:

- Growl under your breath about how angry you are — after the perpetrator has left

- Someone has been annoying you with their behavior for longer than a week

- Caught by a condition or situation that prevents you from moving ahead and it can be corrected

- Tend to talk about your problems only to those who agree with you

Tools for Guidance

These tools will make this positive action step strong and consistent in your life:

Tool 1: Make a list of your expectations on the job. What do you expect in terms of training, compensation, resources, tools, budget, feedback, attention, etc.? Check off the things you're already getting. Take the list into your manager or supervisor and say, "Thanks for those items that are checked, that's what helps me do a good job. Now, for those things that are not checked I'm going to develop a plan to get them and I need your help." Make sure you mention what your boss will get out of helping you do this — more production out of you, a smoother running department, etc.

Tool 2: If you are a manager or supervisor of other people, have your whole team make a combined list of their expectations, check off what they feel they've already got and help them with a plan to get the rest. You may not get everything — but you're moving forward, you're taking action.

Expect ...

Using the above tools you can expect:

- People to take you seriously

- To be more productive in your work

- Ultimately to make more money

- A reputation for being a person of action

Positive Action Step #6: Anticipate

Review

Be prepared for the obstacles others will put in your way, only then can you deal with them without hesitation or uncertainty. Your ability to do this will be evident to others and command their respect. Trying to think on the spot of an intelligent and functional reply to someone who is rude or overbearing will only frustrate you and convince you that you cannot be assertive. A thoughtful, dignified approach to barriers others put up for you requires preparation. If you have an important encounter to handle, write it out. Consider the likely responses from the other person, try out alternative approaches, practice by role playing with someone else or tape recording a rehearsal. If it's important, prepare for it; if it's not, ignore it.

Red Flags

You need work in this area if you:

- Are willing to and do confront others but forget what you wanted to say or get side-tracked

- Want to confront but don't know what to say

- Get very nervous, shake, stutter or stammer when you try to express your position

- Let others intimidate you once you get started

Tools for Guidance

These tools will make this positive action step strong and consistent in your life.

Tool 1: Start with an easy conquest — something or someone you know will be fairly easy to talk to. Plan your conversation, role play and then do it. Your success here will give you strength and encouragement to take on a tougher situation next time.

Tool 2: During your preparation destroy barriers that might prevent you from going ahead, by mentally turning barriers into questions. For example, see how the list on the left could be discouraging as you anticipate your conversation but when it's a question, it empowers.

Barrier:	Question:
"He'll never agree to meet with me."	"How can I make the meeting enticing to him?"
"Why do I have to do this?"	"How will I gain by taking this on?"
"This will never work."	"How can I make sure this has the best chance of success?"
"I'm afraid of the consequences."	"What can I do to make sure my results are what I want?"

Expect ...

Using the above tools you can expect:

- To have many of your assertive conversations go the way you want

- People to listen to you and understand more clearly what you want as results

- A feeling of confidence before and during the encounter

- More actual conversations, not just "wish I had said" and better results when they do happen

Positive Action Step #7: Be Positive

Review

Negative people pull everyone down; they add nothing of value to your work or your life. Avoid them if possible, deal with them assertively if you must, and by all means don't take on their destructive behaviors. The most encouraging point about this positive-negative issue is that it is a personal decision. That is, you decide what perspective you have on any given situation or person. You can choose to be negative or choose to be positive. It is your choice. And that choice is highly consequential because perspective drives attitude and attitude impacts behavior and behavior creates results. Do you want different results? Then change your perspective over which you have 100 percent control.

Red Flags

You need work in this area if you:

- Feel bad about much that's going on in your life

- Are vaguely unhappy or just not completely happy most of the time

- Are dissatisfied with what you have but don't know what you want or don't know how to get it

- Let others pull down your good moods

Tools for Guidance

These tools will make this positive action step strong and consistent in your life:

Tool 1: Answer yes or no to these questions:

1. Do you often dread the day even before you get up in the morning?

2. Do you always expect the worst and are usually right?

3. Do you respond "It doesn't matter" when asked what you want?

4. When hearing good news, do you feel anxious anticipating bad news to follow?

5. Do you believe you could never have a job that is fully satisfying and rewarding?

6. Do you get angry at yourself for making mistakes, missing your goals?

7. Do you work hard but just end up tired and no better off?

8. Do you have lists of things you want to do but somehow never quite get to them?

9. Is your idea of a good time watching TV without anyone interrupting you?

10. Do you find fault frequently with yourself and those around you?

If you answered yes to three or more, you're in a negative slump. Begin implementing the action plans contained in this book and retake this test in 30 days. Keep doing that until you can honestly answer no to all 10 questions.

Expect ...

Using the above tools you can expect:

- Improvements in your results, driven by a new and better attitude

- More production at work and at home, because good attitudes are energizing

- To miss a lot of your old TV programs and not care

- Others to seek out your company and you welcoming it

Positive Action Step #8: Persist

Review

Success goes to those who are willing to make one more try. Don't let another's anger or stubbornness dissuade you from your assertiveness goals. However, also don't persist beyond reason. You can change no one, only influence them. And there are those whom you cannot even do that to! If people do not want to change, if situations are outside your control, if you are dogmatic and insistent, or not truly committed to the effort, chances are you will not be successful. Give up the quest. Place your efforts where you will get better returns. But if others are cooperating, even a little and you are realistic, flexible about time and outcomes and sensitive to the needs of others you could and probably will effect change.

Red Flags

You need work in this area if you:

- Have been working on changing something for a long time with no visible progress

- Your approach is driven by anger not commitment

- Are continuing to do the same thing and expecting but not getting different results

- Feel the reward is not worth the effort or risk

Tools for Guidance

These tools will make this positive action step strong and consistent in your life:

Tool 1: Decide beforehand what your commitment will be to any change you wish to effect in terms of time or money or personal risk. When you reach that limit, consider if you are willing to recommit or move on.

Tool 2: Before taking on any action for change, list the rewards you expect to get and the risk that you will take. If it's not worth the risk, don't do it. If it is, get started. There is no shame in not taking on any assertive task, but there may be regret that you got into it without weighing the consequences. Of course if you do give it up, truly give it up. Don't continue to complain and stew about it.

Expect ...

Using the above tools you can expect:

- Relief, either from winning a hard-fought battle or because of your assertive choice not to fight

- Strength from a proactive decision

- Less stress and anxiety and more positive self-worth

- Exhilaration that you can effect change

Positive Action Step #9: Lighten Up

Review

Focus on the really important things in life. Recognize the difference between a road block and a tragedy; a challenge and a catastrophe. There are few true tragedies for most of us and when they come you know it and there's little you can do. You can accept, you can go on but there is little you can change. But a roadblock is different. That's a problem you can do something about. Leaders know the difference. They focus on the big things and don't let themselves or others get so caught up in the minutiae that they all forget why they are here. Concentrate on that which is vital to your life and the lives of those you care about and are responsible for, then deal lightly with everything else.

Red Flags

You need work in this area if you:

- Don't find many things to laugh about

- Cannot easily list the four or five things in life that are important to you

- Often resent people with light-hearted attitudes

- Will accept nothing short of perfection

Tools for Guidance

These tools will make this positive action step strong and consistent in your life:

Tool 1: Decide right now the three most important things in life to you. Write them down.

1. _____

2. _____

3. _____

Everything you do should directly or indirectly support these three things. Work on that.

Tool 2: Tell more jokes, go to more funny movies, be around children more, smile.

Expect ...

Using the above tools you can expect:

- Your job and your life to be better, more fun, less burdensome

- Better health; even the tradition-bound medical community will agree with that

- To sleep more soundly

- Less tiring work days and more satisfying social times

Positive Action Step #10: Take Care of Me

Review

Leaders take charge first of those things over which they have control. They understand that the basics must be managed first. The areas of life over which you maintain a great deal of control are your physical, emotional, intellectual, social and spiritual health. What you take into your body will support or detract from your ability to move ahead with energy and commitment. Good mental health allows you to think clearly and resist getting bogged down with useless emotional baggage. Competing in this information-saturated culture requires daily infusions of knowledge. You are a social animal. Interacting with others socially is a healthy and worthwhile pursuit. Frequently dipping into your spiritual well will get you grounded in your value system and clarify your priorities. With this control of self, you develop and store the energy needed to handle all the rest.

Red Flags

You need work in this area if you:

- Consistently ingest food or substances that drain rather than add to your physical well-being

- Go to people who will agree with you about your problems but no one else

- Are a learning dropout, that is, you do not have a structured and ongoing learning program in place

- Lack a regular social outlet as a balance to your professional work

- Are not rock-hard clear about your values

Tools for Guidance

These tools will make this positive action step strong and consistent in your life:

Tool 1: Answer the following statements and consider creating a better balance in your life by putting more positive emphasis on those areas where you checked rarely and sometimes.

	Rarely	Sometimes	Often
I get enough sleep.			
I eat a balanced breakfast.			
I exercise regularly.			
I carefully plan my day's activities before I begin my work.			
My work area is organized.			
I am up-to-date on changes in my company's products, services, and staff.			
I take restful and fun days and vacations from work.			

Expect ...

Using the above tools you can expect:

- More control over your life

- Better ability to cope with internal stress

- More structure at work and more fun at play

- Increased control over external conditions

Positive Action Step #11: Have Patience

Review

It took years for you to become all that you are, it will take time to improve and enhance the person you have become. Give yourself time and room to grow. Don't put unrealistic structures on when and how much you should achieve. Concentrate on the fact that you are progressing, and not so much on the amount of progress you have made. Look at others for models on how you would like to develop assertively. Get feedback from those you trust and then share this knowledge and your experiences with others. Mastery is only achieved when we learn, adapt and then teach others what we know.

Red flags

You need work in this area if you:

- Have so many regulations on yourself you are confused about your overall goals

- Don't share what you're learning on a regular basis

- Get discouraged quickly or have impossible expectations for self-change

- Get irritated and give up when you slide back into old habits from time to time

Tools for Guidance

These tools will make this positive action step strong and consistent in your life:

Tool 1: This is called the relaxation technique here but it's also referred to as meditation and has several other names as well. It is an old tool and unquestionably the most functional way you will ever find to enhance your strength and energy for coping with all the demands in your life. Do this now if you can and every day — forever!

Sit or lie down comfortably and close your eyes. Take three deep diaphragmatic breaths in through your nose. Hold for 5 seconds and breathe out slowly through your mouth. Relax all your muscles by concentrating on them starting with the feet, then the legs and so on.

When you are completely relaxed and still with your eyes shut, clear your mind. Put aside current thoughts, problems, and issues and bring into your mind's view a picture of something that makes you calm. For example, a flower or a pool of water.

Stay this way thinking of nothing else for 15 minutes. Your internal clock will tell you when time is up. If you are really concerned about the time ask someone to tell you or set a timer. Be sure you choose a time and place that is free of excess noise and where you will have no interruptions.

Expect ...

Using the above tool, you can expect:

- More creative thinking

- Better listening skills

- More patience with yourself and others

- To be less tired at the end of the day and more energized in the morning

Positive Action Step #12: Be Committed

Review

Commitment can and does change the world. Your commitment to yourself and your willingness to take action on that commitment is the only thing that will keep you moving forward. Assertive leaders are not afraid to make commitments even before they have a complete plan in place.

That's because they know they will put extraordinary effort pulling all the resources under their control into making sure it happens. There are three things you can do with your commitments. You can keep, break or renegotiate them. Which option you choose will determine to a great extent how others view your personal integrity.

Red Flags

You need work in this area if you:

- Frequently break commitments

- Think that any commitment is not important enough to keep

- Only keep commitments to others but not to yourself

- Make commitments only if you are absolutely sure you can keep them; where there is no risk

Tools for Guidance

These tools will make this positive action step strong and consistent in your life:

Tool 1: Complete these two statements:

The one POSITIVE ACTION PLAN (out of 12) where I most need improvement is:

 # _____   Name _____

Therefore, starting today I will take the following action:

_____

_____

_____

Expect ...

Using the above tools you can expect:

- Change

- To begin the process of taking charge of your life

- To feel and be empowered

- The excitement of discovery

(This is a tear-out page. Remove it from your book and post it where you can see it often and follow its messages.)

Positive Action Steps for Taking Charge of Your Life

To live a truly assertive life I must:

1: LIKE ME

The greater my self-esteem, the greater my ability to lead, motivate and persuade myself and others.

2: KNOW ME

Assertiveness begins with knowing my rights.

3: KNOW THEM

Assertiveness is successful when I balance my rights with the rights of others.

4: GROW

When I am willing to take risks, my boundaries are limitless.

5: TAKE ACTION

Only action — consistent, focused action — will get me what I want and deserve.

6: ANTICIPATE

When I am prepared I can deal with any obstacle with certainty and confidence.

7: BE POSITIVE

I have 100 percent control over my perspective — my results are determined by the perspective I choose.

8: PERSIST

Success is often determined by my willingness to try one more time.

9: LIGHTEN UP

When I concentrate on that which is vital to my life and the lives of those around me, my life is a joy.

10: TAKE CARE OF ME

When I am in control of my physical, emotional, intellectual, social and spiritual well-being, all else is manageable.

11: HAVE PATIENCE

I must give myself time to learn and improve.

12: BE COMMITTED

My word is my integrity. Keeping my word announces the value and strength of that integrity to the world.

7 SPECIAL SITUATIONS

"Many can argue, not many converse."

— A. Bronson Alcott

In this chapter we will explore specific situations that you may encounter at work and in your personal life. In each of the case studies, the situations are real. That is, they are all taken from actual conversations that others have shared with me. Use them as models, adjusting and changing the content to meet your unique needs.

In this chapter you will learn how to handle:

- The demanding or autocratic boss

- Managers or supervisors who will not speak in your behalf

- Coworkers who intrude on your ability to work effectively

- Staff members whom you used to work with and who now work for you!

- Negotiating with the team

- Personal encounters with close friends of family members

- A supplier — when you are right!

- Angry customers

- Negative behavior and conversations

Asserting Yourself in Professional Situations

Case Study 1: The Intimidating Boss

Wanda is a systems analyst for a software company. Here's what she told me.

"My boss, Rosalind, intimidates me. I don't think she means to but she has a very powerful presence and a loud voice. When she gets angry I want to dive under my desk. It's hurting my productivity and I can't even imagine asking her for a raise or a promotion. I don't dislike her but I feel my career is in jeopardy as long as I work for this woman."

Since her boss is obviously a direct kind of person, I suggested that a direct approach would be the best. I advised Wanda to get her boss out of her office for this conversation since Wanda may feel further intimidated on her territory. Here's a summary of their conversation

Wanda: "Rosalind, there's something that's been bothering me, even affecting my work, and you could help me out with it."

Rosalind: "What's that?"

Wanda: "You are a very direct person and that's good. Sometimes, however, my reaction is fear and that's not good. I want you to recognize that it's difficult for me to speak up to you. I'd appreciate it if you would ask for my input from time to time and occasionally hold our meetings in my office instead of yours. Can we do that?"

Rosalind was more than willing to accommodate Wanda and told her she knew she was intimidating to a lot of people. She was honest in telling her also that she used that characteristic in her favor but that she didn't want to frighten her own staff! She said she would be more aware of it from now on. Last time I heard from Wanda she said things had improved and the whole office was grateful!

Case Study 2: The "Wimpy" Boss

"Our boss is a wimp," an inside sales group in a jewelry manufacturing firm told me. They said the outside sales department got all the favors, the big bonuses, the annual extravaganza meeting at a posh resort, and company cars. What the inside sales reps got was to keep their jobs and little else. "We work on the same accounts. Sometimes the outside sales reps never even talk to an account but they get all the credit and the commission whenever there's a sale. That's not fair!"

They told me that Roger, their boss, was new in the organization and seen as less powerful than the outside sales manager. He was afraid to go around that manager. When I talked to the reps further, I discovered that although they had approached Roger many times, their approach resembled more whining and complaining than a real and specific request. Here's the synopsis of their resulting conversation with Roger.

Team: "We realize that outside sales is more in favor here than we are. We don't like that but know we can't change it overnight but we can move forward. Here's what we want: a memo to the president when any one of us makes a substantial sale, an annual dinner at a local hotel each year we make quota and a letter to the outside sales manager proposing that we take over the small accounts that the outside sales reps can't visit. We will put this in a letter signed by us so you can just approve it and send it to your boss. Will you do it?"

They got their wish. Roger approved the letter and sent it on. They did get approval for a president's memo and the dinner but not the small accounts. They got something better, however. When they exceed goal, the team receives a monthly bonus now, which can be used however they wish. They got what they wanted this time but not before for three reasons:

1. They gave Roger a list of specific needs instead of general complaints.

2. They took ownership of the project allowing Roger to just approve it, a more acceptable task for someone who doesn't like to take charge.

3. They were willing to start small and work up.

Case Study 3: Promoted from Within

Tim was a lab technician for six years, basically working with the same group of people. He developed what he hoped would be lifelong friendships with some and had some disagreements with others occasionally. Then he was promoted. The ones who were his best friends made unreasonable demands and others who were resentful of his good fortune sabotaged everything he tried to do. When he talked to me, he was ready to give up the position and go back to the ranks. But instead he decided to give it one more try. He called a meeting and said the following:

Tim: "As you know I received this promotion three months ago. At first I was thrilled, but I have run into some difficulties. I want to tell you what I've decided and get your response.

"My job has changed, but our relationship doesn't need to change. In other words, you can like me or not like me — that's your choice. But I will get the job done, so if I need you to do something I'll tell you. If you don't agree I'll listen, make changes if appropriate, but I will make the final decision. I will do your evaluations, hand out the work assignments, prepare scheduling and make all decisions based on your performance and the department needs — not on anything else.

"Does anyone think this is unfair in any way? Does anyone have any problem whatsoever with what I just said?"

Staff: (some head nodding, some low-volume "okays")

Tim: "Good. I want to meet with each of you today to discuss anything you may be reluctant to share with the group."

Tim had a rough time for several weeks. Both his friends and others tested his determination but he stuck with it. Ultimately, he had to let one person go and another left on her own. But basically the team pulled together and Tim stayed their leader. He could have given up but because of that one assertive act he changed the course of his career and his life.

Case Study 4: Coworkers Who Don't Do Their Share

Belinda had a big presentation to give the mayor of her town. Her partner in this project was Beth — or she was supposed to be. Instead, Belinda did the entire report, research, typing and all, with Beth always too busy to help. The day of the presentation, Beth arrived and was irate that, "None of the information regarding my department is included here!" Also, Belinda had not put Beth's name on the report cover. Belinda told me this story after the fact.

Belinda: "Beth, I could have used your input. In fact, the report is really not complete without it. I asked you on numerous occasions to help but you said you weren't available. I don't feel competent to report on your area so I left it out. If you would like to do a separate study, I will tell the mayor when I do my presentation."

Beth never forgave her, Belinda told me. And although her report was good and the mayor appreciated it, he was not happy about the absence of half the study. "What else could I have done?" she asked me.

I told her she did the right thing on the day of the presentation but she may have tried some different approaches before that day. For example, Belinda could have called Beth and warned her. "I am going to submit my department only. When would you like to meet to include yours?"

Or she might have requested a different partner with more time to participate.

Belinda was angry and had a right to be, but her responsibility to the mayor and the project should have taken precedence over teaching Beth a lesson or getting even.

Negotiating Successfully in the Workplace

You are called on constantly to negotiate. You negotiated for the job you have, you may have asked for a raise or a promotion at some time. You perhaps are in meetings where you need to press your view while others oppose it. People negotiate in an organization for the same limited resources. The ability to be successful at this can mean the difference in your getting what you need to do the job and your department to be successful.

In your personal life, you negotiate with family about how to live, raise children, where to go, how to spend your — again limited — resources. Skillful negotiators are successful at work and at home.

There are three cardinal principles for effective negotiation. You will be a skilled negotiator if you are willing to:

1. Suspend your beliefs

Everyone is driven by their own values, paradigms and principles. A shift is rare. So if everyone is busy trying to shove their beliefs down everyone else's throat no one hears and nothing gets done. You can stop that by a willingness to suspend — not give up, not change, simply suspend — your beliefs and listen openly to others.

2. Make tough decisions

Making decisions can be as simple as deciding where to have the annual Christmas party to a life-altering plan to merge departments. Your ability to make decisions will depend on two things: knowledge and courage. Gather every bit of information you can before going into a negotiation and then call on all your courage to make the decision that is best.

3. Be sensitive to the rights of others

Remember the Assertive Belief. Negotiators who bully may get what they want sometimes but a great deal of scheming goes on to undermine the bully. What a waste of time! Also don't forget your own rights. You leave a right to get what you want.

> *Never present your point of view*
>
> *Until you can articulate the others'*
>
> *View as well as or better than they can.*

The following is a very scaled-down version of a negotiation I was involved in recently. Notice particularly the language of Speaker 2.

Jack: "We can't do this; it's too costly and too risky."

Representative: "Is it, Jack? Let's list the cost, the risk and the likely results."

Annette: "I don't care what it costs, everyone's got to be covered by this plan."

Representative: "Who exactly is 'everyone,' Annette, and what do they expect in a health plan?"

Mr. Crowley: "My company has been a role model in this community for 50 years. We're talking about more than our employees, we're talking about the entire business community and all the employees in the town!"

Representative: "Mr. Crowley, how do you think your decision here will affect the larger community?

Notice that the Representative now knows that Jack is concerned with cost, Annette with the employees and Mr. Crowley with his reputation. The Representative represents a sales representative for a health insurance organization. I attended the presentation she gave to sell her services to a bank in a small town in Massachusetts. Now that the Representative has this valuable information, see how she uses it with tact and sensitivity.

Representative: "Let me wrap up with the benefits of the plan I suggest. First the cost of this plan is somewhat higher, but it can be offset by doing this ... Does that make sense, Jack? Is that additional cost something you can live with?

"The plan will cover both exempt and nonexempt employees. It will give more coverage to those employees who are in most need and less to those who need it less. Here's how that works ... Annette, are you still concerned about anyone being left out?

"Finally, it is brand new, a revolutionary way to help businesses provide health care coverage. You can assist other businesses, Mr. Crowley, by continuing to be an example of progress here."

To negotiate successfully you must first get others to express their needs and visions. You are at a distinct disadvantage if all you know is what you want.

Asserting Yourself with Angry Customers

Just about everyone has had to deal with an angry customer at least once. You are not likely to forget the experience. Facing an angry person under any condition can be intimidating, emotionally draining and stressful. Although I will use a customer-supplier scenario here, the points and much of the language can be used in any encounter, personal or professional.

An Eight-Point Plan to Handle the Angry Customer

1. **Acknowledge the person's anger**

   Delay only intensifies the emotional atmosphere and makes reconciliation more difficult. This is not an apology, not yet. This is an acknowledgment that you recognize the customer is angry. Until the other person is convinced he will not listen and will increase the intensity of emotion until you get it!

   "I know you're upset about this, Ms. Bradley. Please tell me what happened."

2. **Listen to the full explanation**

   Even if the customer appears to be rambling, he has often practiced this "speech" and has a need to be fully heard. Studies show that the angriest customer only takes 60 seconds for the initial vent. While this is going on, listen intently, jot down only what you must. You can also take a few deep breaths. Do your best to ignore any sarcasm or demeaning tones or words. Just listen for the facts that will help you solve the problem.

If this is a telephone encounter, don't put the call on hold at this point. That would be construed as an affront the customer is not likely to forgive. If the encounter is in person, look directly at the customer and show by your facial expression that you are concerned. Give short verbal responses.

"Uh-uh."

"I understand."

"I see."

"And then what happened?"

"What time was this?"

3. Make a statement of regret

It doesn't matter whose fault it was, such a statement should be short and to the point and always sincere. The customer is upset and needs your compassion right now. You don't need to take responsibility, just show in words, tone and behavior that you're sorry it happened. This is a brief step but a critical one.

"I'm very sorry about this."

"I feel very bad you had this experience."

4. Tell the person you heard and understood

This can be accomplished by repeating, summarizing or paraphrasing what the person has just said. The other person's confidence in your intelligent comprehension of the situation is paramount here. They need to know that not only did you hear them but that you understand fully. They want assurance.

"Let me makes sure I understand exactly. You sent your July payment on June 23. You then received notice that it was not paid. That notice was sent in August. You now have a large order being

held up for delivery. You have the cancelled check for payment. Have I got that right? Is there anything else?"

5. Stay emotionally tuned in

Although remaining objective is necessary if the problem is to be clarified and solved, you cannot risk an appearance of indifference. Retain an observably caring attitude — in tone, words, posture and facial expressions.

"I know this has some urgency to it."

"I realize your customers are waiting for this product."

6. Find and express a point of agreement

Even if the only thing you agree with is the frustration of the situation, say so. Resist the temptation to find out whose fault it was. Save that for when all the facts are gathered and the circumstances are unquestioned. Even then don't worry about who made the mistake unless it will help you solve the problem or prevent future ones. Studies show the error is with the customer 30 percent of the time. But so what? Make your focus a solution, not blame.

"A notice did go out in August."

"We received that June payment on June 24."

"This is frustrating for both of us, isn't it, Mr. Dawson?"

7. Generate solutions

Tell the customer exactly what you will do, the steps you plan to take. If there is something you cannot do, say so now. Be clear and straightforward. If you cannot solve the problem right then, leave the customer with a clear sense of who will recontact him and when. Tell them what you can do first. If the customer is not happy with your solution, ask him what he would like. You can say no if it can't be done. But professional customer service reps tell me that customers often want even less than they are willing to give!

"I can refund the deposit but I cannot issue credit for your lost business."

"I will speak to the inventory manager and relay everything you have told me. Her name is Barbara Quirk. She will call you by noon tomorrow with a status."

"How would you like us to handle this for you, Ray?"

8. Take action!

Do what you said you would do immediately. No matter how well you treat angry customers, their problems must be resolved as reasonably and quickly as possible to retain their respect and their business. If you must pass the problem to someone else, be sure that person is dependable. If possible, check with them to be sure they followed through. If that's not feasible, tell the customer you are there for them — but never, never create any doubts in the customer's mind about other departments or people in your organization.

"I know Virginia in customer service will get back to you right away, but you can call me as well. My number is ..."

"This problem will get immediate attention here, you can be sure. Feel free to call me any time for a status."

The most important point I can leave you about handling angry customers, or anyone else who is angry, is this: You are not responsible for their anger. You didn't cause it, you can't change it. They are angry because they choose to be. Perhaps you can solve the problem, you can certainly listen, you can make suggestions but you can't change their emotion. Only they can do that. Do what you can do as well as you can do it and then move on.

Asserting Yourself In Personal Situations

Although many techniques for asserting yourself professionally also apply to personal situations, there are some crucial differences. First, the personal situation is likely to be more emotional for both. And, although you may not want to leave your job or alienate a coworker you may take that risk. There is much more at stake with family and friends. Finally since you are apt to know very well how to deeply hurt the other person and they you, the situation requires more delicacy. Tread firmly but lightly.

Case Study 1: When Others Take Advantage of You

A single man in his early forties told me his mother was ill and had come to live with him. Although she could do many things for herself, she wanted him to do everything. She became sullen and irritable if he went out with his friends. He felt trapped. He practiced first and then went home and had this conversation with his mother:

Son: "Mom, I am glad you came to live with me and I enjoy taking care of you. For us to keep our good relationship, however, we must both feel we're happy with the arrangement."

Mom: "You're not happy with me here."

Son: "That's not true. But I am unhappy about one thing."

Mom: "I know you want me to leave. I'll see if I can get a stranger to ..."

Son: "No I don't. But I am unhappy about one thing."

Mom: "What is it?"

Son: "My freedom. When I go out you become angry. You are doing less for yourself now than when you were alone and the doctor says you will feel better if you do more."

Mom: "Oh, what do doctors know! They don't know how I feel."

> Son: "That's true. I would like you to allow me to live my life and to be happy for me and to do what you can for yourself. In turn, I will take care of you and be as good a son as I can. Is it a deal?"

Notice one critical factor about that conversation, the son never let Mom get him side-tracked. She tried several times. He acknowledged each comment briefly and went right back to his point. People with whom we have strong emotional ties often try to avoid what they don't want to hear. It often works because they know our weak points. Follow this as a model and you can prevent that.

Case Study 2: When Children Won't Cooperate

Children offer a unique opportunity for assertive behavior. Since you're the adult you could just demand action. But you've probably learned that doesn't work for long. It is far better to get agreement. This is a very simple and direct conversation I heard a friend have with his four-year-old son.

> Dad: "Jeremy, I've asked you to pick up your toys and you didn't."

> Jeremy: "I want to watch TV now."

> Dad: "Good 'cause I do too. What do you think we need to do first?"

> Jeremy: "Pick up the toys?"

> Dad: "Right. Would you like me to help you?"

The dialogue he had with Jeremy was so simple and yet so clever. He could easily have said, "No toy pick-up, no TV," and Jeremy probably would have given in. But he didn't. Children don't have a lot of rights so if you allow them to make decisions by asking them questions, "What do you think we need to do?" "Can I help?" they get a sense of their own power. As a result, they don't have to show that power in ways that frustrate you like, "I don't want to pick up my toys."

I have the feeling that when Jeremy is a teenager he'll have a more comfortable relationship with adults, thanks to the good foundation Dad is forming now.

Handling Negative People

More productivity is lost and relationships ruined because of negativity than any other single factor. Negative people drain our joy, demotivate teams and families, slow down projects and ruin vacations. Don't let that happen to you or those around you. Learn how to handle, how to be assertive with negative people.

Here are six common negative types followed by sample responses. You can quickly let them know you won't participate in their gloom and doom.

The Critic

This person has a negative opinion about everything, whether you want to hear it or not. No matter what you say or do they know it won't work.

They have done everything you have done and already found out it doesn't work. You don't wear your hair right, make the coffee good enough, do the report well. You can't do anything to please Critics.

"I'm sure there are many ways to do this differently but I like this way and it's my choice."

"Would you tell me exactly how you want this report changed? I have done what I think is best on it already."

The Gossip

This one likes to be the source of information for everybody. All that information is negative, gossip, back stabbing, half truths. They cannot keep a secret. They love to tear down others, particularly those people who are too busy and successful to listen to them.

Gossips love an audience and will look right at you and say, "It's just a little innocent gossip." I'm sure you agree there is no such thing as "innocent" gossip. All gossip is destructive and cruel.

"Does what you're saying have anything to do with our work here? No? Then let's get back to our purpose."

"That's a rather serious accusation. Let's go see him and ask if it's true. No? That's okay, I'll go alone but I'll use your name as my source."

"Did you say Rocco? Why he's my best friend. What were you saying?"

The Martyr

This person is the sacrificial lamb. They walk around with a target on their chest waiting for someone to spear them so they can say, "Poor me."

Martyrs will tell you about every bad thing that was ever done to them. Their primary weapon is guilt. Their favorite phrase is, "Look what they're doing to me now."

"I'm sorry to hear that but it happened two years ago and is no longer relevant to me or you."

"I didn't hurt you intentionally but I'm willing to make amends. Tell me how I can do that. Then we can go on to productive conversations."

"We have all been hurt. However, living a happy and productive life means moving on. Let's do it."

The Cynic

That's the person who must find the misery in anything — the ultimate killer of joy. If the sun is shining, "Gonna burn up my lawn." If it's raining, "This'll drown my flowers." If it's busy, "We never get a rest here." If it's slow, "Probably going out of business."

These Cynics are unhappy, unfulfilled individuals who see life as a drudgery that has to be endured not an adventure to be explored.

"That could happen and it wouldn't be good. What might happen that would be good?"

"That's certainly one way to look at it. And if that will get me what I want, I'll look at it that way too, otherwise I'd like to pursue another line of thought with you."

"That's a good point. What specifically do you think won't work? You could help us prevent a problem here."

The Humorist

This is the kind of humor that isn't fumy. The kind that is sarcastic and hurtful. Jokes that ridicule people's race or sexual preference. Jokes that stereotype men and women. Comments that make everybody in the room laugh at the expense of one.

These people will use anyone or anything for a laugh. They usually have excuses like, "Can't you take a joke?" Or, "Wow, are you crabby today." But they will stop if no one laughs. That's the ultimate cure for Humorists.

"Yes, I can take a joke. Jokes that are funny, not cruel."

"Frankly, I don't find ridicule of others particularly enjoyable conversation."

"If you meant to hurt me, you did. If not, then please don't say that again."

The Put-Down Artist

No one can put you down unless you let them and these folks try their best. They combine a little of the Humorist, unfunny jokes, and a little of the Critic, nothing you do is right. They enhance their own stature by deflating others. Put-Down Artists have the best of everything, you do not and they never let you forget it. If you graduated from college, it was an inferior school. If you won an award, it was easy.

They use sarcasm and manipulative language to tear you down. Don't try to beat them at their own game. They are better at it than you. For example, don't attempt to prove that you are successful or smart or anything else. Go direct with a question as illustrated below.

"Are you unhappy that I won or attempting to minimize my accomplishment?"

"Do you really not like my office or was that an attempt to embarrass me?"

"If you don't approve of this, would you tell me privately? Or was it your intention to get everyone to laugh at it?"

Regardless of the language, you will recognize negativity when you hear it. Use your assertive skills to fend it off but most of all don't become negative. It isn't productive and it isn't fun.

Integrating These Principles into Your Daily Life and Making It Work

Put the Book to Work

Now that you have finished reading this book don't put it on a shelf somewhere to gather dust. You'll have the skills in the book but not in you. Use this book as it was meant to be used — as a catalyst for change. Keep it with you, go back frequently to the sections you found most useful, implement the action plans, practice the dialogues.

Don't let your respect for books keep you from making full use of this one. Write notes to yourself in the margins, bend down the corners of pages you want to refer to later, carry it around in your briefcase, purse or knapsack. Make it work for you.

You Have It All

You have everything it takes to live an assertive life — you always did. But now you have more tools to use. You have 12 positive steps, sample dialogues for dozens of personal and professional encounters, a Five-Part Assertive Conversation Model to use in any confrontational situation, tools and action items for change, exercises for practice, reminder lists, stories and examples to encourage you and provide role models for action and more. You have it all — all that it takes to be assertive and take charge of your life. Good luck!

> *"In any moment of decision the best thing you can do is the right thing.*
>
> *The worst thing you can do is nothing."*
>
> *—Theodore Roosevelt*

INDEX

R
relaxation technique, 111-112
responsibility, 78
role model, 83

S
self-esteem, 28, 14, 15, 28, 93
social life area, 81-82, 109
spirituality, 82, 109
stagehand, 35, 36. See also Behavioral profiles
    interacting with, 43-45

T
technician, 34, 35, 36. See also Behavioral profiles
    interacting with, 40-43
time management, 26-27

V
value system, 82, 109